# REINING ESSENTIALS

# REINING ESSENTIALS

## HOW TO EXCEL IN WESTERN'S HOTTEST SPORT

## Sandy Collier

with Jennifer Forsberg Meyer

Foreword by Al Dunning

Photographs by Caroline Fyffe ✦ Diagrams by Derek Bills ✦ Cartoons by Jim Paul

TRAFALGAR SQUARE
NORTH POMFRET, VERMONT

First published in 2008 by
Trafalgar Square Books
North Pomfret, Vermont 05053

Printed in China

Library of Congress Cataloging-in-Publication Data

Collier, Sandy.
  Reining essentials : how to excel in Western's hottest sport / Sandy Collier with Jennifer Forsberg Meyer ; photos by Caroline Fyffe ; diagrams by Derek Bills.
    p. cm.
  Includes index.
  ISBN 978-1-57076-407-3
  1. Reining (Horsemanship) I. Meyer, Jennifer Forsberg. II. Title.
  SF296.R4C65 2008
  798.2'4--dc22
          2008021665

Book design by Carrie Fradkin
Jacket design by Heather Mansfield
Typefaces: Myriad, Nueva
10 9 8 7 6 5 4 3 2 1

*My sincere thanks to the many great horsemen and friends who have been kind enough*
*to share their knowledge with me,*
*as well as to all the amazing horses that have been my best and most patient teachers—*
*when I've been smart enough to listen.*

# CONTENTS

# FOREWORD

There's a story I love that really applies to horse training. It's about the guy who climbs up a mountain to learn the secrets of life from the "Master." At the top he finds an old man with a long beard, who mostly asks him questions until he eventually figures everything out for himself.

Learning to train horses is a lot like that. You wind up working things out on your own, the hard way, through trial-and-error. Now, however, Sandy Collier has done the up-front work for you. She's spent a lifetime gathering information and techniques from some of the best in the business. Along the way, she used her own God-given talent and intelligence, plus a lot of practical application, to discover which techniques work best and in which combination. She nailed down how to create a truly "broke" performance horse, specifically one that can win in the reining or cow horse arena. Then she put it all into words.

The result is what you hold in your hands. This book contains the essential core of time-tested tips that *actually work*. No matter where you are on the scale of horse training expertise, you'll find insights to inform or refresh your training. I found a lot that sparked my memory, and I'll be sharing various parts of this book with many other people. Everyone I know can benefit from it.

*Reining Essentials* will motivate you. We all want that fire in the belly, and motivation comes from learning. True, the desire to win is also a part of motivation, but more significant is the craving for accomplishment—just knowing that you're getting better and better at what you do. I've written my own best-selling book on reining, yet I still read a lot because I have a passion to learn and keep growing. It's how I stay competitive.

And I'm not alone. One of the greatest horsemen of all time had a sign on the back of his horse trailer that read, "The day I quit learning is the day I die." That was Jimmy Williams, National Reined Cow Horse Association Hall of Famer and world-famous hunter-jumper trainer. His passion for learning was legendary.

Sandy has that passion, too. If you do as well—and you should—you're going to love her book. It's like doing an apprenticeship with Sandy and gaining knowledge from all the greats she's learned from over the years.

I remember when I first met Sandy, about 30 years ago. I could see immediately she was excellent on a horse and gifted with an intuition for training. Some trainers are mechanical; they have "all the moves" but lack that innate knowledge and "feel" that enable them to know what a horse is thinking. Intuition and feel make the best horsemen, as we say, "part horse," and Sandy is like that. She has a keen understanding of the parts of a horse and how they work. She's also analytical and detail-oriented. That makes her fabulous at figuring things out.

As a result, this book is a comprehensive read. You'll find some concepts that have never been discussed in quite this way before. And although it definitely will help you prepare your horse to compete in reining, this book is *not* just about reining. It's about developing a truly broke horse, one that's a pleasure to be around and ride, no matter your discipline.

You'll want your highlighter with you when you read it. You can go chapter by chapter, and when you're done, start over again and advance yourself and your horse even further on subsequent reads. As you acquire more knowledge and ability, you'll get more out of this book each time you read it—because it's deep.

That said, I also found it remarkably straightforward. Sandy has set her ideas forth in a logical, step-by-step way that's easy to grasp. The subheads, photos, and diagrams also help bring everything into clear focus to keep you on track and learning.

And, most important of all, Sandy does right by the horse. She puts his needs first. There are countless examples of that, but here's a particularly good one, from chapter 2, where she explains how to set your horse up to succeed:

"Think back to your school years," Sandy writes. "Did you learn more from the teacher who rushed you, then bullied and humiliated you for a wrong answer? Or from the teacher who set you up to find the right answer, then told you how clever you were when you got it? If you help your horse—instead of hammer on him—when he's confused, he'll start to think of you as a friend he can look to for guidance when the going gets rough."

With this book, Sandy sets *you* up to succeed. Enjoy her insights! They're like eating square meals—pleasing and good for you. I don't disagree with a thing she says, and that's amazing in a book of this length.

*Reining Essentials* will fill you with good ideas and concepts. For anyone who wants to ride, rein, or just get their horses better broke, it's a wonderful learning experience.

**AL DUNNING**
World Champion Quarter Horse trainer and rider, and author of
*Reining: The Guide for Training* and
*Showing Winning Reining Horses*

# INTRODUCTION

In the fall of 1993, I was among those lucky enough to witness the finals of the World Championship Snaffle Bit Futurity. The event, the National Reined Cow Horse Association's finest, was held that year in Fresno, California. During the reined work of the three-part finals, I watched in awe as Sandy Collier and Miss Rey Dry floated through their pattern of circles, slide stops, and spins. Sandy and the filly were smooth, their transitions seamless, their stops and turns fluid yet precise. Miss Rey Dry was flexed at the poll, soft in the jaw, and round over her topline.

The performance looked, in other words, more like a reining run than what it actually was—the dry work of a reined cow horse event. The influence of National Reining Horse Association-style horsemanship was plain to see that day, even though back then it was rare in this type of event. But Sandy was among the few who by the early '90s had mastered the new, more modern style of reining. Her score in the reined work of the Snaffle Bit Futurity finals that year put her and Miss Rey Dry far ahead of the pack. So far, in fact, that

even masters like Bob Avila, Ted Robinson, and Greg Ward couldn't catch up—as they most often did—in the third phase, cow work "down the fence."

And that's how Sandy became the first (and as of this writing, the only) woman to win the world's richest and most prestigious cow horse event. She did it, in large measure, by virtue of her reining finesse.

I wrote a report on Sandy's win that year for the *California Horse Review*, and have written several articles with her for *Horse & Rider* in the years since. Sandy is a journalist's dream—splendid at what she does, plus analytical and articulate enough to tell you exactly how she does it.

In this book, she sets forth her entire training philosophy and method. You'll learn the approach, techniques, and exercises that enable her to consistently produce well-broke, finely tuned performance horses. Colleagues of Sandy admire the way she "stamps" the mounts she trains. Regardless of their breeding or conformation, her horses all have the same look about them—smooth, controlled, correct.

Part of Sandy's success is rooted in basic dressage,

from her three-day-eventing background as a young-ster. That's layered with the real-world school of sad-dle-breaking Spanish mustangs fresh off the range, something she did in young adulthood. Then, in the late 1970s and early '80s, she began expanding her founda-tion to include the wisdom of Tom and Bill Dorrance and their disciple, Ray Hunt. The Dorrance method required "getting inside" a horse's head to present train-ing in a way that's easiest for him to understand. We now know these methods as "natural horsemanship," an approach that has positively impacted horse train-ing in virtually every discipline around the world.

Back then, though, it wasn't readily apparent how to apply these methods to the training of a performance horse. Sandy knew intuitively it was the right way to go, but how exactly did you "get there"? That's what she spent years figuring out and fine-tuning, and what she offers you now, in this book.

I'm proud to have had the opportunity to collabo-rate with her on this project, which I believe will enable you to achieve "the Sandy Collier look"—and success in any endeavor—with your own horse.

JENNIFER FORSBERG MEYER

# PREFACE

## "Master Plan for Success"

I've always wanted to write a book that compiles all the horse-training knowledge I've been fortunate to amass, in order to share it with others. I'm a compulsive learner, ever on the lookout for better ways of doing things. I've learned from every experience I've had—from jumping and galloping cross-country courses as a youth, to breaking wild mustangs, to competing in some of the toughest reining and reined cow horse events in the world.

I've learned from working with great horsemen, from solving problems with the countless horses I've ridden, and from teaching others how to bring out the best in their own horses. Some things I've learned by osmosis, by being exposed to such *true* horsemen that their wisdom and insight couldn't help but seep into me. I've observed all manner of different equestrian disciplines—Western and English—and tried my hand at many of them myself. Along the way, I've learned that "a horse is always a horse," no matter the gear you ride him in.

Always, I've looked for the strategies and approaches that best jibe with the way a horse learns. I've struggled to find which combination of techniques and order of progression will bring the best results—again, keeping in mind the way a horse's mind works. That's because a well-handled horse is a happy horse, and a happy horse progresses rapidly.

Now I present the fruits of my labor to you in this book, and I hope to save you the time and travail involved in the arduous process of learning by trial-and-error! Whether you're a rookie or already well advanced in your horsemanship, this book will help you become better. Think of it as your "Master Plan for Success"—a step-by-step method of creating a well-broke, willing horse to be your partner in this great sport of reining—or indeed, in any sport.

Using my plan will transform your hopes and dreams into specific goals and objectives. I've spelled out *exactly* what you need to do and how to do it. It may take some of the "romance" out of riding a performance horse, but it will compensate by giving you the uplifting—and exciting!—feeling of measurable progress.

As you apply my methods, you'll see how you and your horse are improving *by the week*. This, in turn, will make it easier to stick with the painstaking effort of training. You'll feel your confidence grow as your skills increase. Equally important, your horse will appreciate and benefit from the clearer, surer way you communicate your desires to him.

Ultimately, I can't guarantee you a win in the show pen. But if you follow my advice faithfully, I *can* guarantee that you and your horse will undergo a marvelous transformation.

And you'll have helped me achieve one of my own life goals.

SANDY COLLIER

# 1 PERSPECTIVES

Reining is an addictive sport. I came to it late, having started my riding career in English disciplines (hunter/jumpers and eventing as a youth), and later discovering working cow horses. The cow horses ultimately led to my interest in reining. Once I began learning the nuances of this demanding discipline—in my early twenties—I was hooked.

Reining has been called "cowboy dressage," and with good reason. Like dressage, reining requires you and your horse to interact in a smooth, seemingly effortless way. Your pattern of circles, straight lines, stops, and turns must be seamless; your horse's responses, fluid. Reaching a high level of competency in reining requires a lot of the right kind of practice. In upcoming chapters, I'll be helping you achieve that.

In this chapter, I'll first examine the evolution of the sport, from its beginnings to its current state. Then I'll share parts of my own personal journey, detailing how and why my philosophies regarding horse training have evolved to where they are today.

## Reining's Roots

Reining is an American legacy. On the vast working cattle ranches of the nineteenth century, especially in Oklahoma and California, there were few fences and thousands of cattle to mind. The early working cowboy had need of a steady, athletic mount that could help him with his daily chores—holding and driving cattle, separating one cow from the herd, chasing down a renegade calf. A good horse had to be light on his feet and easy to guide, with quick speed and a handy stop (fig. 1.1).

The cowboy was proud of his well-trained mount, and sought to match him against all comers. This led to informal contests, which were a way to test the handiness and obedience a horse needed to carry his rider through a busy day on the ranch and out on the range.

Later, as the interest in good, working horses spread beyond the cattle ranch, opportunities to show what these horses could do began to multiply. The American Quarter Horse Association (AQHA), founded in 1940, added reining to its official list of classes in 1950. Early patterns were a complicated maze of straight lines,

**1.1** Legacy of the American West
Reining developed in a time when working cowboys needed a steady, athletic mount to help with daily chores on vast cattle ranches. Like this horse, a good one had to be light on his feet and easy to guide, with quick speed and a handy stop.

turns, circles, and figure eights. They required changes in speed, flying changes of lead, rollbacks, sliding stops, and backups.

A watershed for the reining class came in 1965. Inspired by the quality of horses present at an Ohio Quarter Horse show, the judge and contestants set aside the competition's official reining pattern and came up with a new, more challenging one. Bill Horn and Continental King won that class with a performance that left reining enthusiasts everywhere buzz-

ing. By late the following year, the National Reining Horse Association (NRHA) had been founded to promote reining as a sport unto its own.

Under the NRHA, reining exploded in popularity. The NRHA Futurity debuted that same year—1966—and by 1983, the winner's share of the purse was a guaranteed $100,000. In 1985, the NRHA changed the judging system to require the scoring of individual maneuvers within a pattern, rather than the more subjective assessment of an overall run that had been the norm until then.

As refined under NRHA, reining became more stylized, with less emphasis on the sport's ranch-chore roots and more emphasis on a fluid, eye-pleasing run.

In 1986, the NRHA Futurity moved from Columbus, Ohio, to its current home in Oklahoma City, Oklahoma. Also that year, the NRHA Hall of Fame was born, with Dale Wilkinson as its first inductee. By then, reining at the grass-roots level had blossomed across the country, fostering growing numbers of local reining clubs. At the same time, breeders were producing horses specifically for the sport, and competition at the highest levels was becoming tougher than ever.

In 1994, "super slider" Hollywood Jac 86, a grandson of the revered King P-234 (sire of over 20 AQHA champions and some of the finest breeding stock in the country), became the first NRHA *Million Dollar Sire* (having offspring that had collectively earned that amount in NRHA competition). The following year, the legendary Bill Horn became the first *Million Dollar Rider*.

Another pivotal point came in 1998 when reining became the first Western sport to come under the auspices of the United States Equestrian Team (USET). Now an international sport, reining is represented at such events as the USET Festival of Champions and the World Equestrian Games. The ultimate goal is to establish the sport as the first Western equestrian event at the Olympics.

Today's geometric reining patterns require accuracy, fluidity, balance, and coordination from the horse, who is guided with but the lightest touch on a draped rein. He must perform large, fast circles; small, slow circles; flying changes of lead at the gallop; sliding stops; 180-degree rollbacks; and 360-degree spins to the left and the right (fig. 1.2).

World-wide NRHA membership now tops 15,000, with total prize money in 2006 exceeding $10 million. There are 55 NRHA-affiliated local clubs in the US, and another 38 in Canada and abroad.

Why is reining so popular? Because it requires horse and rider to execute a variety of specific movements and put them together in a seamless way that will appeal to both judges and audience. Reining is fun because it's so challenging.

Of course, I knew very little about the finer points of reining when I first began with horses. And, what I did know about breaking and training involved the old-fashioned, rough-and-tumble way. But all that would change when, in my late teens, I left my New England home base and headed west.

## Beyond "Breaking"

After spending time traveling across the country, I found myself at the Tajiguas Ranch, a 3,600-acre avocado and cattle operation in Santa Barbara, California. By then I was in my early twenties, and eventually I was given total care of the ranch's horses, including feeding, grooming, training, and even veterinary work and shoeing. (I still reset loose shoes on my own horses today.)

One of my most challenging projects was saddle breaking a small band of feral Spanish Barbs from Utah. These mustangs were about five years old and had never even been haltered. I'd get one snubbed to a post and bring him hay and water for a few days to introduce myself. In the true "old cowboy way," I'd ease a set of hobbles and sidelines on him, then rub him all over while he struggled, floundered, and repeatedly fell down and scrambled back up.

Eventually, I'd sneak a pack saddle onto him and quickly cinch it up, while he did his best to bite, strike, and cow-kick me. Feet and fur would fly, but when the commotion stopped, the saddle would usually still be on. We'd both stand there for a moment, dripping sweat. Then I'd loosely tie two big salt blocks onto the saddle, one on each side, down low. I'd remove the hobbles, taking care not to get kicked in the head, then untie the halter rope. The horse would tear off and stampede around the pen, head buried between his front

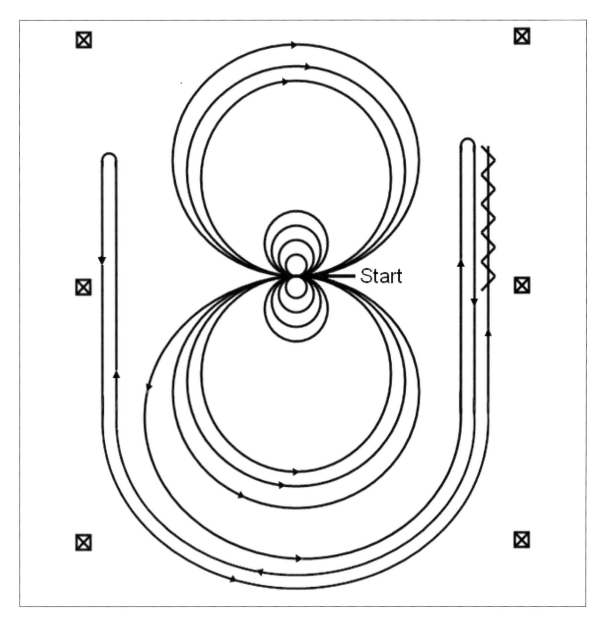

**1.2** National Reining Horse Association (NRHA) Pattern 6

Walk or trot to the center of the arena. Begin there, facing the left wall or fence:

1 Four spins to right. Hesitate.

2 Four spins to left. Hesitate.

3 Pick up left lead, three circles to left—the first two large and fast, the third small and slow. Lead change at center of arena.

4 Three circles to right—the first two large and fast, the third small and slow. Lead change at center of arena.

5 Begin large, fast circle to left, but don't close this circle. Run up right side of arena, past center marker; do right rollback at least 20 feet from wall or fence—no hesitation.

6 Continue back around previous circle, but don't close this circle. Run up left side of arena, past center marker, and do left rollback at least 20 feet from wall or fence—no hesitation.

7 Continue back around previous circle, but don't close this circle. Run up right side of arena, past center marker, and do sliding stop at least 20 feet from wall or fence. Back up at least 10 feet. Hesitate to demonstrate completion of pattern.

Manuever Key

*Circles,* see p. 81
*Spins,* see p. 88
*Sliding stops,* see p. 96
*Backing-up,* see p. 105
*Rollbacks,* see p. 107
*Flying changes,* see p. 118
*Riding a pattern,* see p. 139

legs, bawling and snorting. With every jump, those salt blocks would bang him in the ribs.

That was horsebreaking, cowboy-style, in the early seventies. But I remember thinking, "There has to be a better way!" And, of course, there was. I began hearing about the methods of the Dorrance brothers, Tom and Bill, and their disciple, Ray Hunt. These horsemen advocated "getting inside" a horse's head to train him, rather than wearing him down from the outside. Their noncoercive approach suggested horse training could be much easier on both horse and human than it had been—and whole lot less dangerous.

I was intrigued. I read everything I could find on the topic, attended clinics and, in the mid-1980s, worked with people who knew these methods well. The main thing I learned, the "Holy Grail," as it were, is to "make the right thing easy for the horse, and the wrong thing difficult." No doubt you've heard this popular adage before. It means that if you "open the door" to what you want the horse to do, and simultaneously "bar the way" to what you don't want (by making it uncomfortable or difficult), the horse will generally choose the option you desire.

It sounds logical, and it does indeed work. But it's not always obvious exactly *how* to make the right thing easy in a way that makes sense to the horse. I've spent the last 25 years figuring out how to do this, as well as how to apply these ideas and methods to the training of a performance horse (fig. 1.3). My specific strategies are what I'll share with you in upcoming chapters. In chapter 2, I'll take a look at how horses think and learn.

**1.3** Noncoercive training methods
Back in the day, I knew how to break a horse "cowboy style," but I kept thinking, "There has to be a better way." Since the early 1980s, I've been figuring out how to apply the methods of Tom and Bill Dorrance and Ray Hunt to the training of performance horses, like Trailena, an amazing cowhorse.

# 2 TERMS & CONCEPTS

Horses don't think the way we do. With our bigger brain, however, we can compensate for that and present our training in a way that makes it possible for the horse to understand and respond. In this chapter, I'll explain how horses learn, describe my own approach to training, and define the basic terms and concepts I'll be using in the chapters that follow.

## How Horses Learn

Horses are basically lazy. They'd rather be under a tree somewhere, swatting flies off their buddy, than lugging us around an arena. Given two choices, they'll always opt for whichever is less work. Knowing this, you can stack the deck in your favor. You do this by making the option you want more desirable (again: easier, more doable, more comfortable) than others, giving the horse a chance to volunteer the correct "answer," then praising him lavishly for it.

This noncoercive approach encourages him to think and respond rather than simply react (the latter being his natural way). In effect, it enables him to *learn how to learn*. He discovers he can work his way through situations, becoming confident so he can always find a way out of discomfort. Once he realizes this, it can even be fun to watch him go through his repertoire of responses, hunting for the one you're looking for.

All this doesn't happen quickly, however. In a typical learning session, your horse will give you several wrong answers before hitting on the correct one (fig. 2.1). For example, when you're teaching him a turn on the forehand, the first time you put your leg back to ask him to move his hip over, his initial response will almost certainly be to sling his hip into your leg, trying to push it away. When that doesn't work, he'll likely try stepping forward. And when that doesn't work either, he'll go back to pushing into your leg, or maybe even crow hop or kick at your foot.

Finally, on the fifth or sixth try, he'll step away from your leg, just as you intend. So reward him with a pat and a break, then ask again. His first response this time will almost certainly be wrong again—probably pushing against your leg or stepping forward. But his

**2.1** Getting the right response
**In a typical learning session, a horse will give you several wrong answers before hitting on the correct one. Your job is to be clear, consistent, and patient. It takes time. Here I get Catty to "soften her face" by asking for a couple steps back.**

resistance and resentment—a raised head, a stiff back. A good way to remember this is a terrific quote from trainer Doug Williamson, "When a horse's head is up, his brains dribble out and down his neck, where it's impossible for him to use them."

Another way to think of this is that the horse learns by the *release of pressure*, rather than by the application of it. If (for some crazy reason) you want to teach your horse to put his head in the air and run every time you pull on the reins and kick with your heels, all you have to do is pull and kick until he takes off—then release all pressure from your reins and legs. Your horse will understand that when he responds to a pull and kick by running off, he is "rewarded"—the uncomfortable cuing stops.

Now let's look at the best ways for us to use all this information about how horses learn.

## Riding Smart

Training horses is not supposed to be mortal combat. We are expected to be smarter than they are. (If the reverse were true, they would be "riding" *us*, right?) Ideally, we use our bigger brain to make learning seem doable and feel nonthreatening to the horse.

Here are the rules of thumb for "riding smart" that I've accumulated over the years.

You can't train a horse that's hurting, so rule out physical pain. Whenever your horse is being stubbornly resistant, make sure it's not because he's in pain.

- ► Is he not stopping well? His hocks may be sore.
- ► Resisting a spin? His suspensory ligaments (the structures supporting the back of the lower leg) may hurt, or he may have bumped his knees together, making them tender.
- ► Tossing his head? His teeth may need floating.

Always check with the appropriate expert—a veterinarian, farrier, chiropractor, or equine dentist—to

second or third try will probably be correct. He will have skipped all the other wrong answers.

Do this for a week, and he'll not only get it right the first time, every time, but he'll also step smartly and smoothly around a full circle and be totally relaxed while doing it. But...it takes time!

Keep in mind, too, that horses are easily frustrated and discouraged, so you must be extremely patient and consistent in how you present learning opportunities. If you get impatient, lose your temper, or make the learning curve too steep, your horse will start to worry. He'll become nervous and his adrenaline will flow. He'll chew the bit, grind his teeth, or wring his tail. He'll "stutter"—become quick and desperate in his responses.

The horse learns nothing in these situations. Any correct response you happen to elicit at this point, under duress, likely cannot be repeated. When you gain your horse's cooperation through intimidation, that cooperation is always defensive, and accompanied by

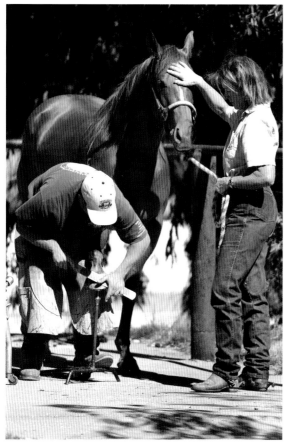

**2.2** Importance of soundness
You must make sure your horse receives the best possible shoeing from a competent farrier. You owe that to him, and besides—you can't train a horse whose feet are hurting.

**2.3** Always training
You're either training or "untraining" your horse whenever you're with him. If you're leading him, make him lead properly. All the random moments you spend together add up to a lot of good training time. Trailena respects my space and walks quietly at my side, making him safe and pleasant to handle.

rule out a physical problem whenever you hit a roadblock (fig. 2.2). Only after you get the green light should you push on with your training. To head off problems, I have my horses checked regularly by my vet—I don't wait until one starts resisting.

Maximize every moment. Whenever you're with your horse, you're either training or *untraining* him (fig. 2.3).

▸ If you're picking out his feet and he's dancing around or leaning on you, don't let him get away with it. If you do, you'll set an "I'm the boss" prece-

dent in his mind. Instead, take the time to set his priorities straight by insisting that he stand obediently when you ask.

▸ If you're riding him through a gate and he won't move laterally off your leg, school him until he does.

▸ If you're going down the trail on a pleasant morning and he's pulling on the bit, don't think, "Oh, it doesn't matter now." It does!

All these random moments add up to a lot of good training; don't waste them.

Set him up to succeed. A horse must understand and accept an idea before it can become his own, and only then can you train him how you want him to do it. Another way to think of this is that you must *show him* until he understands and accepts a maneuver, and only then *train him* on it (fig. 2.4). It's a subtle but important distinction. And only when he *gets it* can you go on to ask for speed. If you push for speed while he's still confused, he'll come to resent what you're trying to teach him, or at the very least become badly rattled.

So use your aids in a way that enables your horse to *find* what you want, rather than forcing him to do your bidding. Yes, hauling on the reins is one way to get a horse stopped. But it is much better to lope him until he's a bit tired, so that when you pick up your reins he *wants* to stop. Help him figure it out, and give him time to do so, then reward him when he does the right thing. Your horse must have confidence that if he needs a moment to think something through, you're not going to get all over him for it.

Once he's figured out the *what*, only then can you start teaching him the *how*. To use the stopping example, that includes getting his hind end up under him and not leaning on the bit while he does it.

Think back to your school years: did you learn more from the teacher who rushed you, then bullied and humiliated you for a wrong answer? Or from the teacher who set you up to find the right answer, then told you how clever you were when you got it? In the same way, if you help your horse when he's confused—instead of hammering on him—he'll start to think of you as a friend he can look to for guidance when the going gets rough.

Be a contrarian. This goes along with *training every moment*. If your horse wants to do one thing, make him do the other.

- Is he leaning in one direction? Make him go the opposite way.

- Is he "amped up" and wants to lope? Make him stand still for a moment.
- Does he want to stand? Make him lope.
- Is he eager to be at the front of the line? Put him at the back.

Don't let him train *you*, either. If he's a spook, don't forsake trail rides—go on lots of them and get him exposed to all those frightening things. Don't make excuses for him. By being a contrarian instead, and insisting he do what *you* want rather than what *he* wants, you're continuously reinforcing that *you* are the boss, not he. Horses crave leadership, and if you don't provide it, they will.

Train both sides. Whether you know it or not, you own two horses, a *right* horse and a *left* horse, and they both need to be trained. Never assume something you've taught your horse to do using one side of his body will translate to the other; it won't! You must train both sides individually. If he can shut a gate working off your left leg, also teach him to do it off your right. Each side will likely require slightly different approaches, because most horses are a little stiff (resistant to bending) to the left and hollow (bend excessively) to the right. More on this when I talk about vocabulary in a moment (see p. 15). Ultimately, you'll spend about the same amount of time working your horse to each side, striving to make his stiff side more flexible, and his hollow side more evenly bent.

Be precise. A horse's brain is like a computer, so the old "garbage in, garbage out" admonition applies. With a computer, if you enter a command that's just one letter off, the computer won't recognize and perform the command. Similarly, if you want optimal performance from your horse, you must ask for a movement exactly the same way each time. Sometimes we get frustrated with a horse that's not responding correctly. We think, "You dummy—you did it fine yesterday." But our horse

**2.4** Show your horse what you want

You must set your horse up to succeed by always showing him unambiguously what you want. Only when he understands and accepts an idea as his own can you train him *how* you want him to do it. As I ask Catty to bend to the right, I take a firm feel of the right rein and "pick up" her right shoulder by twisting my right hand, palm up, close to her neck (like putting the key in the ignition of your car and turning it). I pull my left hand out to help her stay round and keep the circle symmetrical, while my left leg is positioned just behind the front cinch to keep her rear end aligned and my right leg is at the cinch to encourage her to bend around it.

is thinking, "Yes, but I'm confused, because you cued it differently today." A fully trained horse is often able to fill in for a miscue, but while he's still learning, the more precise and correct you can be, the faster and more reliably he'll learn. Good stuff in, good stuff out.

Develop great timing. Remember, horses learn from the *release* of pressure (reward), not the application of it. And when you release, your horse will associate this reward with whatever he was doing *immediately before* the release. So if you're a split second late releasing, you're confusing your horse and slowing his learning, or even inadvertently "rewarding" something else entirely. If you're asking for a step backward, the instant he even begins to *think* "back," you should lighten the reins for an instant as a reward, then resume asking. But if you miss that moment, and instead lighten as he's raising his head or opening his mouth, you're rewarding him for what you *don't* want. *Timing is everything.*

Be consistent and fair. A cue can't mean one thing half the time, and something different the other half just because you don't enforce it. If you're inconsistent in your follow-through, you oblige your horse to choose whether you really "mean" it each time you ask. That gives him only a 50-50 chance of doing the right thing. Inevitably, he'll choose the easier, and in most cases, wrong thing and get himself in trouble. This inconsistency on your part is like "lying" to your horse, but you *must* be honest to gain his trust.

Similarly, you must never lose your temper. When you do need to make a correction, it must always fit the crime. Never suspect that your horse is trying to be bad on purpose—he isn't. You've probably confused him, so take that into consideration in your response. A scared and intimidated horse isn't going to try for you. But if he understands that you'll always be fair with him, he'll get confident enough to give his all. That said, don't hesitate to "raise your voice" if that's what's needed.

Solve—don't create—problems. Any time your horse doesn't respond the way you want, don't compound the problem (or create a new one) by taking a hasty or overly aggressive approach (figs. 2.5 A & B). Let's say, for example, your horse is getting racy instead of staying in the steady lope that you've asked for. You really feel he should be "getting it" by now, but instead of losing your cool, you simply take all slack out of the reins, then draw him to a trot, then a walk, then a stop, then a backup—all in about six or so strides. Then sit for a while and give him a chance to relax, and try that lope again. If, instead, you jerk him into the ground, scaring him, the next time he's going fast, he'll start worrying about getting jerked, and the problem will have been compounded.

In other words, when you do it the correct way, he thinks, "Oops, I'm racing along here...now she's picking up the reins to break me down...I guess I'll 'give her my face' and come to her, because I know she'll insist on that, but then at least I get to stop and rest." But the

**2.5 A & B** Creative problem-solving

When your horse isn't responding the way you want him to, strive to solve the problem creatively—don't cause a new problem. If, for example, your horse gets "racy," leaning on the bit as Cody is in A, don't jerk him into the ground and scare him. Instead, find another way to get the job done, and avoid the fight. In B I use the fence to regain Cody's attention and slow him down. This way, instead of learning to brace his jaw and fling up his head, he learns that although I insist on having my way, I'm not going to traumatize him in the process.

other way, he thinks, "Oops, she's picking up the reins and she's going to 'rip me a new set of lips'...better brace my jaw and get my head up to protect myself." See how that works?

Be systematic. Don't try to teach your horse something when you haven't laid the foundation. Also, don't get into an argument you don't have the tools to win. Before you ask your horse to move laterally, for example, you must first be sure he understands the concepts of giving to bit pressure and moving away from pressure on his sides.

Go back to get ahead. Start every schooling session by asking your horse for something he already knows well and feels comfortable doing. Then, after he's shown you a few times how good he is, sneak another little bit of teaching in there. For example, go back to walking that good circle before you ask for that little lateral step. Break all teaching down into small bits, always returning to the last thing your horse did well (especially if he gets confused), then inching forward from there. This keeps him in a positive frame of mind for learning.

Be creative. I usually try to teach my horses something a certain way, but if I'm not getting through by the third attempt, I take a different approach. In other words, I won't *force* a horse to learn something "my way." Let's say I'm asking for the transition from the large, fast circle to the smaller, slower one, and my horse won't slow down. I can lope him until he *wants* to slow down, then reward that thought. This works with many horses, but if it doesn't with the horse in question, I may try breaking him down to a trot, then to a walk, then to "Whoa," and rest. I may also try pulling him into a circle to slow him down. Or, as a last resort, I may be a bit more punitive and aggressive in my request for a downward transition, and then back him up to reinforce my point.

Ultimately, you must figure out what works for each horse, as horses learn differently. Some trainers have a "my way or the highway" mentality. When a horse fails to respond, they say, "This horse doesn't 'fit' me." What they're really saying is, "I'm not very creative."

*Ride the horse you're riding.* This means, although you're working from a plan, you're also quick to change that plan depending on how your horse feels and responds on any given day, or in any given moment. In other words, be open to what your horse needs to work on, as opposed to what you'd planned to do. Say, for example, you'd intended to work on stopping one day, but when you started riding, your horse wouldn't move off your leg. You should change your game plan and work on sidepassing and other lateral exercises until your horse does become responsive to your leg, then resume your original plan.

Also, don't expect your horse to be able to do something just because his dam or sire did it, or because you saw someone else doing it with a similarly bred horse. Concentrate on the unique individual that is your horse, and ride accordingly.

*Be realistic in your expectations.* This applies both to your level of expertise and your horse's ability and level of training. In other words, don't try to do something you don't know how to do, or that's way beyond your horse's understanding. In determining what your horse is capable of, you must consider not only his current level of training but also his breed, his conformation, his age, his level of maturity. (I'll talk more about this in chapter 3.)

*Accept 1 percent improvement a day.* This doesn't sound like a lot, but think of it this way: in 100 days, you've got 100 percent improvement. That's significant progress, yet very doable. Let's say on one day your horse makes

---

### ■ One Layer at a Time ■

Training a horse is like painting a car. You've probably seen one of those incredible "show car" paint jobs—where the smooth, rich color looks as if it's 10 feet deep. Here's how that's done: after the foundation is perfect, with all the blemishes filled with lead and sanded smooth, the painter applies a primer, which he also sands until it's perfectly smooth. Then comes the first color coat. After that's dry, the painter will sand it until it's almost entirely gone; just a few molecules of color remain.

Then he applies the second color coat, lets it dry, and sands it until just a blush of color remains. He'll do this 20 or more times, building up the color just a few molecules at a time, over a period of many days, until it's as clear and as deep as an Alpine lake.

Well-broke horses are made the same way.

---

a little breakthrough in his stopping. You can ask him for that same level of stop a couple of times to reinforce the learning, but don't keep trying to improve it further on the same day. That way, your horse begins to think, "Hey—I'm quite a little stopper!" But if you keep after him to do even better than what he just gave you, he begins to think, "I'm *still* not getting it! I must be a terrible stopper." He gets more and more anxious, and any gain you made disappears. Accept that 1 percent, then ask for another 1 percent tomorrow.

*View everything in proportion.* Don't become fixated on any one part of your horse's body, or any single exercise, or any specific training goal to the exclusion of everything else. For example, don't put excessive importance on your horse's headset at the expense of his ability to move laterally, or be collected, and so on.

Get outside input. Ask a knowledgeable friend to watch what you're doing and provide feedback. I've had friends say, "Why are you doing *that?*" when I didn't even realize I *was* doing it. Go to clinics, and write down what you learn so you can work on it at home. Watch videos of yourself schooling or showing. (A quick word about those show videos: we tend to buy only the ones where we had good runs, but the ones we most need to analyze are those showing weak runs. That's where we need more work!)

Know when to get help. Use the various forms of feedback you have to help you know when to turn to a professional. Everyone's threshold for this is different. Obviously, if your horse is behaving in a way that scares you, or if what you've diligently tried is just not working, hire a trainer. You may need only a few corrective sessions to get back on track. People tend to wait until problems have escalated and they have a big expensive problem on their hands, when they could have paid $30 or $40 and been straightened out in an hour. As with your car, it's better to get a tune-up every now and then rather than wait for the darn thing to break down.

It's okay to work your horse. Everything I've said about being fair and reasonable and flexible is true. But I don't want you to get the impression that you can't ask your horse for his best effort. People often feel guilty about pushing their horse, or about making him work when it's cold or it's feeding time or it's late in the day or whatever. Don't! Think of it this way: what if you saw a help-wanted ad that said, "Job opening. Two square meals a day and a comfy room provided; housekeeping services included. Full medical benefits. Pedicure and new $125 shoes every six weeks. Applicant need work only one hour per day." Wouldn't you want that job? I sure would. So when you're riding your horse in that one hour per day, don't be afraid to ask him to *work* (fig. 2.6).

## A Working Vocabulary

Now let's define some of the key terms and training concepts I'll use throughout the book. Some of these concepts have become fully understood by trainers only in the last few decades. Before that, we were still able to make many good horses, mostly because a good horse tends to be good in spite of what we do to him. But just imagine how much better those horses could have been! And think of how much better your horse will be, once you have a fully loaded "tool box."

Between reins and legs: Imagine your horse is in a box created by your hands and legs. If he pushes his nose out, he bumps into the front wall of the box—your hands. If he bows out or falls in, he bumps into one side of the box or the other—your legs. And if he gets strung out, his hind end hits the back of the box—both of your legs driving him forward. When he's between the reins and your legs, he's easily guided in any direction, free of the influence of magnets (see p. 19).

Breaking down: A nice, soft, gradual downward transition through the horse's gears (lope, trot, walk) resulting in an eventual stop or backup.

Comparison to *drawing the horse into the ground:* A slightly more punitive break down, involving more rein pressure and quicker transitions from the lope to the walk to the backup.

Comparison to *setting the horse down:* This is the most extreme action, reserved for punishing the horse or regaining his attention when he is completely ignoring you and pushing through the bridle. Here, you aggressively pull the horse "into the ground," demanding an immediate stop or backup.

Broke horse: A horse whose individual body parts can be put wherever you want them, at any time, without resistance.

**2.6** It's okay to work hard

When you're riding your horse in that one hour per day, don't be afraid to ask him to *work*. Dually and I practice backing-up with energy and power. He's showing good effort, giving his face and shifting his weight back on his haunches as he responds willingly to my cue.

Collected or "framed up": Your horse is "soft in the face" (yielding to bit pressure), and engaged behind (working with his rear end well under him). His back is lifted and rounded, allowing his center of gravity to shift back a bit, lightening his front end to allow freer, more athletic movement and greater responsiveness to your hands.

Defiance: Your horse's willful challenging of your authority by saying "no." You must handle *defiance* dif-

Theories abound as to why horses tend to be stiff to the left and "too-bendable" to the right. These include the way they were positioned in their mothers' womb; the asymmetrical distribution of their internal organs; and the fact that we handle them more from the left than from the right.

But the hypothesis that makes the most sense to me has to do with eye dominance. Most horses become left-eye dominant as they mature, meaning they prefer to see things predominantly through their left eye. This requires a slight tweak in their atlas vertebra (at the base of the skull) to tip the head fractionally to the right, bringing the left eye more into play. That's balanced by a slight "S" shape to the neck, followed by other offsetting corrections in their shoulders, rib cage and hips, all of which wind up making them stiffer to the left.

Sounds plausible, but who knows? Ultimately, it doesn't matter why horses tend to be this way. What does matter is that we do our best to get them "evened up." I'll talk a lot about this in upcoming chapters.

ferently from how you handle *resistance*. Meet defiance with firm and decisive action.

Comparison to *resistance:* Stiffness in body and mind that causes a horse to avoid doing what you ask of him. As just emphasized, you must handle *resistance* differently from *defiance*. Meet resistance with lots of educated riding to soften and supple your horse.

Direct rein: Using the rein on the same side as the direction you are traveling or turning (i.e. in a *right* turn, the *right* rein is the direct rein) It moves the horse's nose in the desired direction so the body and feet can follow.

Comparison to *indirect rein:* Using the rein on the opposite side of the direction you are traveling or turning (i.e. in a *right* turn, the *left* rein is the indirect rein), often via pressure against the horse's neck.

Dropping a shoulder: Your horse is not keeping both of his shoulders upright and even, causing a lean or drift to one side. A dropped shoulder can make your horse change his front lead at the lope, "leak" in turns on a cow, stop and back up crookedly, or knock down a barrel. Many of the exercises I do are all about keeping the shoulders up and even, or what I call "standing them up" when one or the other has dropped.

Foundation: The basic training of a horse, to be laid "brick by brick." You begin with the simplest things your horse can understand, then add one new task at a time. You must return to the foundation—the basics—often, to review them and set the stage for additional learning. You should also go back to basics any time your horse becomes confused or overwhelmed. In this way, you gradually expand the envelope of what your horse can willingly, easily do.

Hiding: Your horse is trying to avoid something that's become daunting and scary. When he gets in trouble too many times for the same thing, he becomes confused and frightened, and he begins avoiding even "going there." If he comes to dread spinning, for example, he'll resist even looking in the direction of the spin. It's much easier to keep "hiding" behavior from developing than it is to gain a horse's confidence back and erase such behavior.

Hollow: A tendency for the horse to bend or soften excessively while going in one direction. Horses tend to be hollow to the right and stiff to the left. When you lope your horse to his hollow side, it feels as if he's bending much more than the arc of the circle; however, his inside hind leg is moving to the inside of the circle to avoid carrying weight, causing his neck, shoulders, and rib cage to drift to the outside of the circle.

Comparison to *stiff*: Difficulty in bending or softening while going in one direction. Horses tend to be stiff to the left and hollow to the right. When you lope your horse to his stiff side, he resists bending on the arc of the circle (his nose is *not* to the inside of the circle, nor does he have his inside shoulder up and a soft bend from poll to dock). He carries his inside hind leg more up underneath him, or engaged, but he'll feel as if he's always cutting in on his circles when going this direction. You'll usually feel more "comfortable" loping on this lead (to his stiff side), as he's tracking straighter and will usually stop better, but that doesn't make it his better side. It's as challenging to supple the stiff side as it is to straighten the hollow side.

Comparison to *straight*: Traveling with the hind feet in the tracks of the front feet, and the neck and spine aligned and straight (on a straight line) or curved (on a circle). Horses tend to be asymmetrical in the same way people are right- or left-handed; this makes them travel differently depending on whether they're going to their stiff or hollow side (fig. 2.7). Many of the exercises in this book will be aimed at making your horse more symmetrical.

"Hunt the circle" or "hunt the stop": Part of "riding smart" is finding ways to make your horse *desire* to do the things you want to do. Teaching a horse to "hunt the circle" is teaching him to *desire* to be on the circle—loping that circle is the place he'd like most to be, and in fact, he *volunteers* to be on the circle and stay there with little or no guidance from you. Similarly, "hunting the stop" is creating *desire* in the horse to stop at the subtlest signal. This is accomplished by using the stop as a reward and making it a good place to be—and keeping it that way by never punishing the horse during the maneuver.

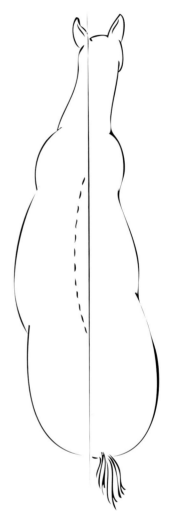

**2.7** The asymmetry issue

**Horses tend to be asymmetrical in the same way people are right- or left-handed. Here is a drawing of a "typical" horse traveling on a straight line: his head and hind end tip to his "hollow" right side, while his stiffer side bulges to the left. This natural asymmetry makes him travel differently depending on which direction he is going.**

"Key in the ignition": The lifting, twisting motion made by one hand to lift and pick up the horse's shoulder on that side. It's similar to the motion you make when turning the ignition key in a car with your right hand. The motion causes the thumb to turn 90 degrees, bringing the palm to face upward, which in turn brings the rein closer to the horse's neck.

Magnets: Objects that attract your horse's attention and therefore draw him to them. A horse's body goes where he looks, and he looks where his mind is. Predictably, this is the gate, the barn, the trailer, where his buddies are, and so on. Magnets are what make straight rundowns, symmetric circles, and on-the-spot spins problematic. To overcome this effect, you must become more important to your horse than his magnets are. Many of the exercises we'll do are designed to "break" the pull of magnets.

Off the bit: In the sport of reining, it is ideal for the horse's head to be just behind the vertical and the rider should feel little to no contact with the horse's mouth. This signifies that the horse is off his forehand, with more weight being carried by his hind end, and that he is "giving" or "soft in" his face (see also Collected or "framed up.")

On the same page: Describes a horse tuned in to the rider, rather than operating on his own agenda. He waits for the rider's instructions and is willing to be guided—he's thinking and responding, rather than reacting. (To learn how the NRHA defines it for the benefit of judges, see p. 146.)

Panic point: The reaction of a horse when you've failed to clearly explain what you want, yet continue to "demand" by pulling or kicking. The horse can't find a "safe" direction in which to go, becomes anxious and claustrophobic, and rears, runs off, flies backward, or engages in some other out-of-control, evasive behavior. If, by contrast, you realize his brain is heating up and you "toss him a rope" (by going back to the last thing he really understood and inching forward from there), he'll calm down and consider you his friend—one he can turn to in times of need or confusion.

Shoulder resistance: Your horse is using his shoulders to avoid doing what you've asked him. My Australian friend and true horseman Gerald O'Brien says a horse "makes a fist with his shoulders," and he's dead-on. The shoulder is where most of a horse's resistance is played out (see also Dropping a shoulder). Think of your horse's shoulders as an iceberg you must keep chipping away at to get freer, more responsive movement.

# 3
# THE RIGHT HORSE, THE RIGHT GEAR

To succeed in reining, the horse you ride and the equipment you use must be right for the job. In this chapter, I explain how to evaluate your current horse to see if he's suitable for a career in reining and give you some pointers for finding a new mount if that's what you need or decide to do.

I also talk about the equipment you need to successfully train and compete in this sport.

## The Horse You Ride

The specific qualities of the horse you ride are absolutely key to your success in this sport. If you're a beginning rider, especially, you should work with the best trained, "best minded" horse you can afford. Nothing takes the place of a forgiving, well-trained mount, especially if part of your goal—as I'm sure it is—is to have fun.

That said, many people come to a new sport with a horse they're fond of, and perhaps can't afford or don't want to "trade up."

On the pages that follow, I discuss the must-have characteristics for a reining horse, and you can use this information to help you decide if the horse you now have is up to the task, or to evaluate prospects if you decide to trade up—now or in the future. Later, I also provide a few specific tips about breeding your own reining prospect (see p. 26).

### Breed, Age, Sex

In general, the best reining horses are Quarter Horses, or individuals of other breeds (such as Paint or Appaloosa) that have a lot of Quarter Horse blood in their pedigrees. For an amateur getting started in reining, I recommend a middle-aged (that is, seven to 15 years old) gelding. Mares can also make good mounts, but tend to be a little more variable in their moods as a result of hormonal cycles. Stallions come with their own set of additional challenges and are best left to the pros.

### Mind

The horse's mind or disposition is absolutely crucial. *Your horse must be quiet*. That means he lopes on a loose rein and doesn't get "motored up" easily. We call this a "pedaler," as in pedaling a bicycle. A pedaler goes only as fast as you "pedal," and he coasts when you stop pedaling.

Your horse should also be at least willing to *try* to do as you ask, and the more forgiving he is, the better. You're going to make a lot of mistakes along the way. A horse that gets mad and holds a grudge, remembering the bad things during future rides, is an unnecessary challenge.

It's much easier if, when you make a mistake, you can say to your horse, "Oops—didn't mean that. Delete!" and he'll forgive and forget. (You'll know from riding him whether the horse you now own is such an individual. To assess this and other disposition characteristics in a prospect you're considering buying, it's best to get the opinion of an expert—more on that in a moment.)

### Conformation—What You Want

Great horses come in all shapes and sizes. There are, however, some conformation traits that will make your job easier, and some that are particularly tough to deal with if your goal is reining. Let's talk about the positive things, first.

Overall balance: In my opinion, this is the most important characteristic to look for in a reining prospect. Whether tall or short, heavier or lighter boned, when viewed from the side, the horse should seem balanced in his body mass: he shouldn't have a big, burly front end that doesn't match his hindquarters, or a croup that's higher than his withers. A balanced horse will ride better, stay sounder longer, and be a more attractive mover (figs. 3.1 A & B).

Head: Most important is the eye, which should be large and kind. Horses with a prominent, "soft" eye are usually smarter and gentler than those with average or smaller eyes. An overall nice-looking head, with fine features and small ears, won't contribute to the horse's ability, but will always make him easier to sell if and when you decide to trade up.

Throatlatch: Best if it's clean, meaning relatively sleek and open as opposed to thick, "meaty," or coarse. A horse with a clean throatlatch finds flexing at the poll more doable, and therefore is easier to "frame up" and keep collected.

Neck: A long neck with a nice curve to the crest makes it easier for the horse to use his neck in balancing the rest of his body.

Withers: These should be well-defined and fairly prominent; otherwise your saddle will roll around or slide forward all the time.

Back: Shorter is better, as a compact horse is typically quicker and finds it easier to gather his hindquarters under him, where you need them to be.

Hindquarters: These are a horse's engine and brakes. Well-developed hindquarters make it easier for him to balance himself on his hind end, and to stop. Ideally, the croup should not be overly steep, and the deeper the hip (meaning the length from the point of the hip to the gaskin), the better for strength and propulsive power.

Chest: Best if it's well-developed but not too bulky. If the chest is too wide or muscle-bound, it's harder for the horse to spin and move laterally. On the other hand, you don't want both front legs to look as if they come out of the same socket, or the horse won't be balanced laterally.

Front legs: Viewed from the front, they must be straight, as legs that form a sturdy column of support are more likely to stay sound carrying the horse's weight. A little toeing-in is not as bad as a little toeing-out; with the former, the horse can still spin and is less likely to interfere than is the horse with splay feet.

**3.1 A & B** Good vs. poor reining prospects
*Good:* The Quarter Horse in A has excellent conformation for a reining horse: body parts proportionally balanced; hips deep and well-muscled; legs straight, with hooves of the right size and shape; front pasterns angled about the same as his shoulder. A horse built like this has a good chance of performing well and staying sound. *Poor:* Though she has a powerful hind end, the mare in B is built a little "downhill"—her hips are higher than her withers. Plus, her front pasterns have quite a bit more slope than her shoulder; matching angles are best for long-term soundness.

Viewed from the side, front legs should, again, look like straight, sturdy columns. A horse that is back at the knee or has feet obviously in front of the line of the leg is predisposed to lameness. The angle of the pastern should roughly equal the angle of the shoulder for best movement and soundness.

Hind legs: From the rear, these should look fairly straight. A bit cow-hocked is acceptable, but if the hocks turn in too much the horse won't be able to slide without awkwardly splaying his legs.

From the side, the hind legs should be set under the horse, but not too far (camped under). Nor should they be too straight (post-legged), or he won't be able to get deep into the ground. Riders used to prefer their reining horses have really straight hind legs to help them slide a long way, but in those days the horses didn't break at the loin, bringing their hind ends under and stopping deep the way we want them to now.

Hooves: These should be healthy, well-formed, and large enough to support the horse.

**3.2** Conformation to avoid
This mare's long back will make it relatively hard for her to gather her hindquarters under her. Her ewe neck, which causes her high head carriage, makes it difficult for her to flex at the poll and lower her head without falling on her front end.

## Conformation—Specific Flaws to Avoid

Any horse, no matter how built, can be made better with the right training, but some conformation faults limit a horse's ability too much, making your job too difficult and frustrating.

With that in mind, here's what you should specifically avoid in a reining horse.

Thick throatlatch: The horse will find it difficult to flex at the poll, and therefore be constantly fighting your hand when you ask him to soften.

Ewe neck: Also called "upside-down" neck; it makes for an unbalanced horse (see fig. 3.2). If in spite of his natural inclination to resist lowering his head you are able to get his head down, he'll fall on his front end.

Long back: A little too long is okay, but a really long back tends to be weak, which makes it difficult for a horse to get his rear end up underneath himself (fig. 3.2). He'll be hard to collect, as there's just so much more to get gathered up.

Overly leggy: Horses with too-long legs just seem to have their feet too far away from their brains! Such horses aren't solid-feeling; they're wobbly.

Too-big feet: A nice, large hoof is one thing, but an overly large foot is another, and causes clumsiness in various maneuvers, especially rolling back and spinning.

## Shopping Tips

If you don't have a horse to ride, or if you've determined the one you do have isn't right for the job, you'll have to acquire one. Taking a horse on loan, or leasing one can be helpful while you're learning, but it's more likely you'll need to purchase a horse for this purpose.

And, as you progress in the sport, you may find a need to move on to a horse with more talent. Here are some tips for finding a horse to suit your needs.

Get help! This is by far the most important advice I (or any knowledgeable professional) can give you. Using the guidance and counsel of a reputable trainer to help you locate and evaluate a suitable horse will save you untold amount of time, money, and grief. It may be the trainer you work with now, or someone you retain specifically for this purpose, but you need a person to evaluate your abilities and match you up with a mount.

Trainers typically have an extensive network of contacts, and often know about horses coming available before they hit the market. They can also spot flaws that you'd otherwise miss—that is, until the horse is purchased and performing poorly! They know the weak spots of many of the reining horses already on the market, and can make an assessment of what you can live with—and what will sabotage your efforts to learn the sport.

If you don't follow any of my other advice, do follow this recommendation: Get help finding a horse!

Value your first impression. Your initial gut reaction to a horse is extremely important, because horses are what they seem. Is he quiet to handle, friendly, and curious, or is he skittish or cranky? Does he seem to like people, or would he obviously rather be left alone? Be especially careful of falling for a pretty face, such that you overlook clear warning signs.

Specifically, don't make excuses for any questionable behavior ("I must have approached her too quickly—that's why she spooked," or "He was probably cranky because it was feeding time"). Be doubly cautious if the seller tries to offer such explanations, or the old standard, "He's *never* done *that* before."

Bottom line: any traits you notice when you first see the horse when your mind's a clean slate accurately represent who the horse "is." Those traits aren't going to change, and they'll be a common thread throughout all the horse's behavior. Be cautious.

Buy the individual, not the "brand." It's true that certain traits seem to carry through in bloodlines, so a horse with a lot of successful reiners in his pedigree may have a higher likelihood of success than a "nobody." Still, my advice is to shop for popular breeding, but *buy* the balanced, good-minded individual. Your advisor will be able to guide you in this area.

Get a prepurchase exam. When you've found a horse you think will work for you, a prepurchase exam or "vet check" is a must to be sure the horse has no health problems or conformational flaws.

For example, flexion tests (where the veterinarian holds the leg in a flexed position for a set amount of time before having the horse trot off) can reveal a lot of potential joint problems.

If the horse isn't too pricey, and if his flexion tests are negative, you might forego having his legs X-rayed; make a decision on this after discussing it with your trainer or advisor and the vet. Radiographs can be useful in revealing joint and bone problems that may worsen over time.

## It Ain't So

MYTH: I need a "push-button" horse.

Actually, I don't believe I've ever met this breed! What people are usually referring to is simply a well-trained horse. But, without a well-trained and competent rider, this horse won't stay "push-button" for a day. Horses always meet us on our level, and if it means they have to drop down to do it, they will.

The good news, though, is that a well-trained horse can usually be "rehabbed" quite quickly. In other words, he can be tuned up again readily if his inexperienced rider does "untrain" him (as usually happens). So, for all these reasons, I recommend you buy a horse with the most training that you can afford.

If you decide you can only afford one set of radiographs, make them of the horse's stifles. OCD (osteochondritis dissecans), a condition that results from a loss of blood supply to an area of bone beneath the surface of a joint, is increasingly seen in our perfor-

Finding a good horse is one thing; keeping him healthy and happy is another. There are books, courses, and seminars devoted to this topic, and you should become as educated a "horsekeeper" as you can. Here are some tips to get you started.

**Go "quality":** Get the best help you can find in your own local area—the best trainer, veterinarian, farrier, hay supplier, whatever. Good help and advice is invaluable, and saves you time, money, and anguish in the long run.

**Provide checkups:** Have your horse seen regularly by your veterinarian to make sure he's not developing a problem or becoming sore in a muscle, tendon, or joint. Checkups by a qualified equine dentist (this might be your regular vet or someone else) are also a must, both for overall health and the horse's comfort and responsiveness in the bridle.

**Use a good farrier:** Maintain your horse on a regular, five- or six-week schedule with the best farrier you can find who is familiar with shoeing reining horses.

**Feed and supplement well:** Buy the highest-quality hay available in your area; if you have doubts about nutrient value, have the hay tested. Balance your horse's nutrition with a good vitamin/mineral supplement and a joint supplement (check with your veterinarian on what will be best for your horse).

**Provide turnout:** Horses are happiest when they can "be horses" at least some of the time, and that means as much turnout as possible. A large pasture for running and grazing is ideal; an arena or paddock is better than no turnout at all.

**Use good equipment:** Buying the right gear at the start—high-quality pieces that fit your horse properly and perform well—will go a long way toward keeping him happy in his work (see Gearing Up, p. 26).

**Cross-train:** Focusing on reining exclusively will burn your horse out mentally. Work cattle, play with ground poles, ride down the trail—anything to mix it up a little and keep your horse's mind fresh.

**Give him a pat:** Handle your horse like a good working dog—not a pet, mind you, but a valued part of your team—whose contribution you respect and admire. Let him know you appreciate him.

---

mance horse bloodlines, and when in the stifles it is career-ending. So although bone spurs on hocks and even some changes to the navicular bone in the foot can be managed with the right kind of ongoing care, stifle problems are a deal-breaker.

I prefer to X-ray the hocks and feet as well. Not only do these radiographs reveal potential problems, hav-ing them on hand may also be an advantage when you go to sell the horse down the road. Let's say that, after conferring with your advisor and the vet who performs the prepurchase exam, you decide to buy a horse with a manageable problem that showed up on a radiograph, such as some small lesions on the navic-ular bone. When you later go to sell that horse, if you can demonstrate the problem hasn't worsened significantly (by comparing the radiographs the buyer gets to the ones you had done when you bought the horse), the sale will probably go through.

### Breeding Tips

Breeding your reining prospect has its own set of unique challenges, and you should become as familiar as you can with what's involved before you choose this option.

That said, if you do decide to go the "homegrown" route, use the best mare you can find. Ideally, she'll have either won money in reining competition, or have produced foals that are money winners—the latter being the best indicator of her likelihood of producing a good prospect.

Also, breed her to the best stallion you can afford that's had a lot of success in the reining pen. A long, successful show career is preferable to a one-time win, no matter how big, as it's indicative of soundness and a good mind as well as talent. And, as with the mare, a stallion that's already sired talented reiners is a more proven and marketable commodity.

As for bloodlines, the popularity of various lines comes and goes. I could name a bloodline that's hot right now, as I write this, but by the time you read it, we'll have moved on to the next favorite. In any event, get as close as you can to the current "A-Team." A son of a son just isn't the same as the guy himself. Similarly, even full brothers and sisters can be as different as night and day, so don't assume, without the proof of progeny, that siblings will be as successful in the breeding shed as their illustrious relative.

## Gearing Up

In this section, I talk about the gear you need to train and show in reining. I also describe the equipment necessary in the training exercises in this book, plus touch on some of the specialty items available for dealing with specific problems.

---

### ■ THE Bit to Know about Bits ■

A bit is meant to communicate your desires to a horse, *not* force him to respond. My approach to bits is fairly simple, and my tack room doesn't contain a huge variety of them (though all the bits I do own are well-constructed and well-balanced). I'm not a gimmick person, and when things start to fall apart, I go back to basics (and a plain snaffle) instead of going to a "bigger bridle."

Yes, bits are a key component in the horseman's tool box. But they must never substitute for a thoughtful, patient approach to any training problem.

---

### Snaffle Bits

I use a smooth snaffle with "O" rings to start my two-year-olds (fig. 3.3). A plain snaffle like this is extremely forgiving, and its "signals" (the way it communicates the action of your hand to the horse's mouth) are relayed across the tongue and on the corners of the mouth, making them easy for a horse to understand.

As time goes on, if a horse gets dull or I find I need more control of him, I may move up to a slow or "lazy" twisted-wire or regular twisted-wire snaffle (fig. 3.4). The twists in the mouthpiece provide a bit stronger action than smooth snaffles; slow or "lazy" means not as many twists, thus a milder action than a regular twist.

I also use a gag snaffle from time to time (fig. 3.5). Gags are designed so that the bit slides up in the horse's mouth when strong pressure is put on the reins; this also creates some poll pressure. With these actions, a gag can be used in small doses to help soften a horse that persists in leaning on the bit when you ask him for more collection.

In general, I stick with snaffles until all the horse's basics (essentially, chapters 5 through 9) are solidly in place. Experience has taught me that if a horse has stiff or unresponsive spots due to lack of training, a stronger bit not only *doesn't solve* the problem—it generally *makes it worse.*

Ideally, you should maintain your horse in a snaffle for all the exercises in this book, right up to the section in chapter 10 on "putting him into the bridle." (To clarify, it is common reining parlance to use the term "bridle" when referring to a headstall featuring a shank bit, and "snaffle" when it features a snaffle bit—although of course both are bridles as most riders understand them to be.) This is true whether your horse is two years old or ten. Then, when you put him in a transitional shank bit, go back through all the exercises and do them again, now keeping your hands closer together, moving more as one.

## Shank Bits

Because they have shanks added to the mouthpiece and a curb strap, these bits provide leverage that applies pressure to a horse's chin, tongue, bars of the mouth, and poll, and sometimes the roof of the mouth, too (depending on the shape of the *port*, or curve, in the middle of the mouthpiece). The main reason to move to a shank bit is to gain more collection and precision (fig. 3.6). I'll talk more about this, as well as the process of using transition bits to move from a snaffle to a shank, in the section on putting your horse in the bridle in chapter 10.

## Reins

There are two basic types of reins: split and romal. Split reins (two long, separate reins) are most common and tend to be "user friendly"—unless you happen to drop one! Split reins are sometimes referred to as "Texas style."

Romal reins, a continuous loop with a "romal," or extra length, attached (think of the letter "Y") are more often seen in California (where they descend from the

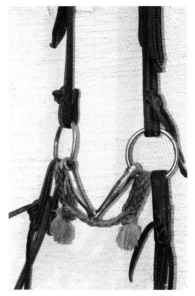

**3.3** Ring snaffle
A plain, smooth-mouthed snaffle with "O" rings—the standard for colt-starting and back-to-basics tune-ups. This bit is forgiving, and its "signals" on a horse's tongue and lips are easy for him to understand.

**3.4** Twisted snaffle
A twisted-wire mouthpiece gives this snaffle a slightly stronger action. This is a regular twist; I also sometimes use a "slow" or "lazy" twisted snaffle with fewer twists and thus a milder action.

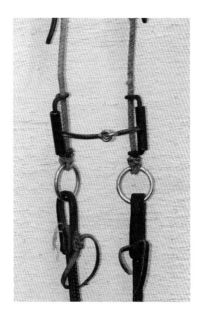

**3.5** Gag snaffle
This bit is designed to slide up in a horse's mouth and create pressure on the poll when the reins are pulled. Used in small doses, it can help soften a horse that persists in leaning on the bit.

**3.6** Shank bit
The shanks (cheek pieces), port (curve in the mouthpiece), and curb strap on this "bridle bit" provide leverage that applies pressure to a horse's chin, tongue, bars, and poll. I provide photos of the different types of shank bits in chapter 10.

**3.7** Regular noseband
**Also called a cavesson, this can be used to help a horse that "gaps" his mouth. Although it won't cure the gapping, it enables the action of the bit to be more precise.**

A

B

**3.8 A & B** Dropped noseband
**The horse in A is wearing a dropped noseband, properly adjusted. Because it is fastened *below* the bit, I believe the dropped noseband is more effective than a regular one. Another advantage of using the dropped noseband is that it never combines with the bit to pinch a horse's lips the way the regular noseband in B will as I increase rein pressure.**

vaquero tradition), especially on cow horses. They are sometimes referred to as "California style."

### Nosebands

Some trainers use a noseband (also called a cavesson) on all their horses; some never use them at all. I use one on horses that "gap" their mouth in an attempt to escape the action of the bit (fig. 3.7). The noseband won't cure a horse of gapping, but it will enable the action of the bit to be more precise.

I prefer the dropped-noseband style, as this type never pinches the lips between it and the bit. Being positioned and fastened below the bit, it also tends to be more effective (figs. 3.8 A & B).

## Martingales

A running martingale (with rings through which the reins are threaded) must be adjusted properly in order to be effective, as in the photos (figs. 3.9 A–C). When it is correct, it can be highly useful early in training in keeping a horse's head in the "control range." That is, it only comes into action when the horse raises his head above a certain height. Think of a running martingale as "training wheels": use it only when you feel you really need it, and be sure to remove it as soon as you've gained adequate control.

A standing martingale, which attaches to a noseband and physically prevents a horse from raising his head above a certain height, is not a training device and is better avoided. Draw reins, which can force a horse's head down and in through a pulley action, can also easily wind up doing more harm than good. Unless you're working with a professional to guide you when dealing with a specific problem, you should not use them.

## Saddle

You need a well-made and well-balanced saddle, and it won't be cheap! The good news is that you can train and show in the same saddle, so if you take good care of it, you only need one (fig. 3.10).

What's important in a reining saddle is that it allows you to be close to the horse's back (i.e., the saddle isn't built up in the seat so that it sets you high and away from the back); the stirrups swing freely and don't force your leg forward or back; and you can sit in the center of the saddle's seat (the front isn't built up in such a way that forces you back toward the cantle).

**3.9 A–C** Running martingale

**This training tool helps keep the horse's head in the "control range" by preventing him from raising it too high. The reins are threaded through the martingale's rings, which—when correctly adjusted—create a slight downward pull on the bit *only* when the horse raises his head higher than desired in the earliest phases of training (A). To properly fit a running martingale, adjust the length so that the rings of the fork just reach to the horse's throatlatch (B), or so they reach to his withers (C).**

**3.10** Appropriate saddle
**A well-built, well-balanced saddle enables you to feel "close" to the horse's back. I prefer to use a cutting saddle, like the one shown here.**

Apart from these considerations, I recommend you ride in as many different types of saddles as you can, until you sit in one and say, "Ahhhhh." (Naturally, you want to be sure it fits your horse well, too.)

Cutting saddles are my favorite, and Calvin Allen's in particular; I just trade in the oxbow cutting stirrups for 2-inch flat-bottoms. I prefer the rigging—which stabilizes the front and back of the saddle through the attachment of a cinch or cinches—to be 7/8, as that fits a wide range of horses. The mass-manufactured trees used in the majority of custom-made saddles these days fit most horses, but if your horse has high withers, a really round back, or some other conformation extreme, you'll need to pay closer attention to fit. Ask someone knowledgeable to help you.

### Pads

There's a lot of marketing pressure from advertisers these days to buy an expensive pad. Plan to invest a bit to purchase a good one, but don't be misled by this hype—again, ask someone to help you. Look for a respected brand name and quality material, and make sure the pad's not too thick or too thin (it should protect your horse's back without changing the balance of your

### It Ain't So

**MYTH: A switchy tail is the result of using spurs.**

It's true you can irritate a horse by constantly pecking at him with your spurs—even make him cranky enough to use his tail. But spurs alone aren't usually the cause of a switchy tail. His genes play a huge role in his behavioral patterns, and can include a predisposition to "express himself" with his tail.

■ **Arenas, Round Pens, and Other Work Spaces** ■

You usually have to make do with what's available to you, and even the smallest training space can be creatively utilized. But in a perfect world, bigger is better. Anything larger than 100 feet by 200 feet is heaven! I am fortunate—my track covers a half acre, and my big arena is 150 feet by 300 feet.

The footing of your work space is actually more important than its size. Three inches of sand on a base of well-tamped clay or decomposed granite is good. Be sure it's watered and groomed so there's some cushion to it. Your horse will be happier, stay sounder, and slide farther.

saddle). For showing, you can layer a handsome saddle blanket over a wool underpad—something that coordinates with your show shirt if you want to get fancy.

### Spurs

Spurs are an important tool as they give your leg cues a higher degree of precision. As with the bit, the purpose of using spurs is for precise communication, so application is light, not forceful. Think of an artist creating a painting—does he use a house-painting brush or a fine-tipped art brush? Properly used, spurs enable you to be as precise with your cue as that artist is with his brush.

When I reprimand a horse with my spurs, I do it quickly and with the degree of pressure dictated by the misbehavior in question. Without spurs, the same degree of correction would involve so much kicking that *that* might actually irritate the horse more!

One caveat: be sure you have an independent seat—no gripping with your lower leg to stay on (I'll talk more about this in the next chapter)—before you start wearing spurs. Jabbing your horse accidentally as you struggle to stay seated won't speed your training program one bit!

Most horses respond well to a blunt, 10-point rowel (fig. 3.11). This can be applied to the horse's side directly or rolled against his barrel with good effect.

**3.11 Adding spurs**
Once you have a truly independent seat, you can use spurs to communicate your cues more precisely. This blunt, 10-point rowel can be pressed or rolled against the horse's side with good effect.

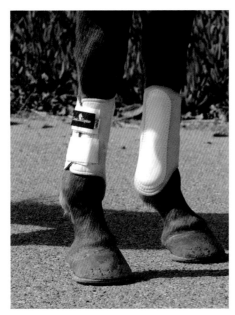

**3.12** Splint boots
These protect the front legs from injury due to "brushing" (when a hoof or shoe from one front leg strikes the other front leg) and also shield the front tendons from a blow from a hind hoof.

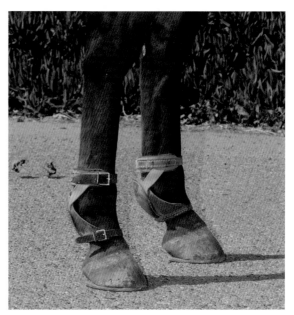

**3.13** Skid boots
These are important as a horse begins to progress with sliding stops. The boots protect the back of the hind fetlocks from getting burned when sliding along the ground.

## Protective Boots

I use splint boots on the front legs of all my horses every time I ride or work them (fig. 3.12). They protect a front leg from a blow from the other front leg, as well as protecting the tendons from a blow from a hind leg.

Bell boots are necessary only if your horse tends to overreach with his hind legs thus hitting the heel bulbs of his front legs, or if he bangs his coronet bands when spinning.

Using skid boots becomes necessary as your horse progresses in his sliding stops (fig. 3.13). These boots protect the back of the hind fetlocks from getting burned by friction created when the hind legs slide on the ground.

Knee boots are valuable when spinning if your horse hits the front of one knee with the bony protrusion on the back of the other knee (fig. 3.14). Without protection, a horse can become quite lame from this.

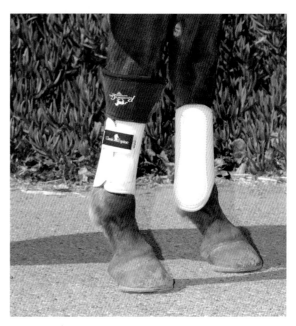

**3.14** Knee boots
When a horse tends to hit one knee with the other while spinning, a knee boot will help to avoid his getting injured. Make a homemade version by adding an upside-down bell boot to one splint boot—usually only one knee needs to be "booted," like this.

# $4$ RIDER BASICS

To progress in reining or any equine sport, you must be able to communicate effectively with your horse. To do *that*, you need to have certain mental and physical skills as a rider. Your body and brain must work in unison to create a well-balanced package.

Mentally, you must be able to maintain a teaching atmosphere in your practice sessions (as opposed to a confrontational one), and set your horse up to succeed (that is, make him think what you want is *his* idea).

Physically, you must be able to maintain an effective position in the saddle and use each of your body parts—hands, seat, legs—independently of the others.

In this chapter, I explain each of these concepts by looking at the various "working parts" of the rider. I also give you suggestions for improving your overall effectiveness in the saddle.

## Your Head

Our human brain is what puts us at the top of the food chain, so to speak. As a goal-oriented rider, you must make best use of your brain at all times. It sounds obvious, but it's not always easy. Specifically, you must:

Control your emotion: Deal with your horse the way you would a six-year-old child, never expecting more than he's reasonably able to deliver at any time. Explain things clearly, using alternative explanations as necessary and "taking the time it takes" to get your point across. Never become frustrated and "lose it"; it's unfair to your horse and only sets training back, anyway.

All this requires superior mental and emotional control on your part, but without it you'll never be a superior horseman, and you'll never draw the very best from your horse.

Be analytical: Use your brain to make what you want easy and rewarding for your horse, and what you don't want uncomfortable (I'll talk more about exactly how to do this as I go forward). Think of your approach as "equine judo"—you're using your horse's strength to your advantage, and redirecting its flow as necessary. Success is when your horse doesn't even realize he's been redirected! As I said earlier, he believes it was his idea from the start.

Plan ahead: Make sure the lesson you're intending on any given day is one your horse is ready for (i.e., you've already set the foundation for this lesson on previous days). Then, before the lesson, prepare your horse for success. Would he benefit from being turned out or longed? (You want him fresh enough to respond, but not so fresh that he's bouncing off the arena walls!) Make sure he's wearing the gear you need for the lesson planned—perhaps a running martingale, a smooth-mouthed snaffle, and skid boots?

Be realistic: Don't try to teach your horse something that's over his (or your) head. Remember what I said in chapter 2 about looking for no more than 1 percent improvement each day. This super-moderate approach makes learning very doable, and will boost your horse's confidence. The progress you'll make adds up more quickly than you might imagine.

## Your Seat

How you sit in the saddle affects all your body parts. If your seat is incorrect, it will hamper you from using your hands and legs properly. Your seat must be:

Well-positioned: Imagine a plumb line dropping from your ear, falling through your shoulder and hip, and passing just behind your heel. Sit on the triangle formed by your pubic bone and seat bones, tucking your rear end under just a bit (fig. 4.1).

Avoid the "chair seat," which, when seen from the side looks as if you're sitting in a chair, with your legs propped out in front of you (fig. 4.2). Also, avoid a "perched" position, where your upper body is too far forward, and you're sitting primarily on your crotch and not your seat bones (fig. 4.3).

Sit quietly, avoiding "body English"—exaggerated leaning and "pumping" to ineffectually prompt your horse to do something he would already be doing if the cues were clear. Body English not only looks bad, it also "tells on" us. We tend to lean to where we know the horse *should* be (amateur cutters do this a lot), but the action makes the horse lose balance and actually go the opposite way. As an example, when you lean back to stop a horse, you're actually driving him forward.

Balanced: Use your internal sense of balance (as honed by lots of time in the saddle) to keep you in the proper position, rather than gripping with your legs or hanging on the reins (see Your Hands, below). Good balance frees you to have good legs and good hands.

Active: Use your seat to reinforce your other cues. For example, drive with your seat in combination with leg pressure and clucking to prompt forward movement, increase speed, or encourage your horse into the bridle. Sit deep and relaxed to "draw your horse to you" and slow him down while still driving his hind end up under him.

## Your Hands

Soft, educated hands are the "mark" of a horseman. A beginner's hands are fast and harsh, and often used to maintain balance in the saddle—a cardinal sin! By contrast, good hands are:

Independent: Strive to maintain your body's position entirely from your seat, legs, and internal sense of balance, leaving your hands free to operate exclusively as a means of communication.

Well-positioned.: Position your hands thumbs-up when holding the reins in two hands, or with romal reins in one hand. When holding split reins in one hand, your palm should be facing downward, with your index finger separating the two reins (see fig. 10.8 A. p. 132).

**4.1** Correct basic rider position

I'm sitting so that if a line were to be dropped from my ear, it would fall through my shoulder and hip, and pass behind my heel. My weight is on the triangle formed by my pubic bone and seat bones, with my bottom tucked under.

**4.2** Incorrect—"chair seat"

I'm slumping in a "chair seat," and I'm sitting too far back on my bottom, with my legs too far out in front of me.

**4.3** Incorrect—"fetal crouch"

I'm assuming the "fetal crouch" position that causes my legs to grip and ride up, and my weight to come out of my heel and off my seat bones. I end up being "perched" too far forward.

The line made from the bit to your elbow should always be straight so your hands are neither too high nor too low (figs. 4.4 A & B). This should be the case whether they're being held passively or pulling for a stop or turn. Don't pull down!

Precise: Strive for precision. That little "give" in the reins when you reward a correct response must come immediately after that response, or your horse won't connect the two. (Remember, a horse links the very last thing he did *before* a reward or a correction *to* that reward or correction—and nothing else.) Precision and timing are critical.

Coordinated: Your hands should almost never work alone. Use them in conjunction with your legs to influence your horse's direction, and with your seat to slow your horse down or speed him up. You'll find coordinating your hands to your legs and seat easier to do at slower speeds, so don't be in a hurry to go fast.

Feeling: Strive for "feel" by keeping your hands light and thinking about what your horse's mouth actually *feels* like through the reins. Do you feel him pulling on the bit when you take the slack out of the reins? Do you get periods of contact intermingled with nothing at all? Your goal is for the horse to be "off the bit" and light in the bridle so that the connection between your hands and his mouth is no more than a faint, but consistent pulse of energy, and for most people sensing and maintaining this takes practice.

Learn to discern the length and evenness of your reins without looking down at them. Don't focus on your horse's head for feedback as you attempt a maneuver: *feel* his response through the reins (and your legs and seat—more on that in a moment).

The most educated hands are invisibly "attached" to the horse's feet and can keep them moving freely, evenly, and in the right direction via the subtlest of cues.

**4.4 A & B** Correct hand-to-elbow position
There should be a straight line from the bit, through your hand, to your elbow, at all times—when in "neutral," pulling back to stop, turning, or asking the horse to "give his face" (A). Most importantly, never pull *down*. Maintain the straight line from the bit to your elbow at all gaits, including the lope (B).

## Your Legs

Although your legs are partly what secure you in the saddle (along with your seat and balance), you must be able to use them as needed (one leg or both together) to communicate with your horse. For this to happen, they must be:

**4.5** Correct foot placement
**My foot is correctly positioned in the stirrup—not jammed all the way "home." My ankle is softly flexed, with 30 percent of my weight on the ball of the foot—the contact point with the stirrup. The rest of my weight sinks into my heel.**

Independent: Don't grip with your knees or calves. Use your legs together (in a squeeze, bump, or kick), to tell your horse to increase speed or move up into the bridle; and use them individually to tell your horse to step laterally or straighten out a crooked body part.

Well-positioned: Let your legs drape naturally down around your horse's barrel, keeping them relaxed and free to be used as needed. This position is the opposite of the "fetal crouch" often seen with beginning riders whose legs grip and ride up on the horse's sides, with the heels up and toes down (see fig. 4.3). Your legs should be just a tad ahead of the vertical—so that, again, a plumb line from your ear would fall through your shoulder and hip and wind up just behind the back of your heel. The ball of your foot should be the contact point with the stirrup.

Ankles soft: Roughly 30 percent of your weight should be on the ball of your foot, with your heel sinking downward (fig. 4.5). Keep it a soft, flexible pressure, though, to enable your ankle to be a shock absorber that helps keep you from bouncing.

## It Ain't So

**MYTH:** If you're inexperienced, you'll ruin your horse by attempting new exercises.

It's true that if your horse is well-trained but you're not, he'll eventually meet you at your level of expertise. But don't let it keep you from trying. A horse with a solid foundation can always be sharpened up to his original level of training by an expert so long as you haven't spoiled him (i.e., allowed him to become "balky" and disobedient). Naturally, if your horse has no foundation or basic training, then you're in uncharted territory where it's easy to get offtrack and hard to get back on. As I said in chapter 3, a green horse with a green rider is never my first choice.

**4.6 A–C** Use of spurs
**To roll your spur, bring the rowel in close (A), then press it into your horse's side and flex your ankle to roll it along his side (B & C). This can be a subtle or obvious cue, depending on the pressure you apply.**

Where and how you apply leg pressure dictates how the cue is interpreted by your horse. I'll describe the "where" first, then we'll look at the "how."

The three cueing zones are *neutral position, in front of neutral*, and *behind neutral*.

The *neutral position* is where your legs naturally rest, with your heel just a bit in front of that plumb line I've talked about. It's right behind the cinch area. If you apply one leg in the neutral position, you're controlling your horse's rib cage, for example, when you ask him to bend through his body on a circle.

If you apply one leg 2 or 3 inches *in front of the neutral position* (that is, right *at* the front cinch), you're controlling the shoulders as you do when you help him get started in a spin.

If you apply one leg 2 or 3 inches *behind neutral position* (that is, a bit farther back on his barrel),

you're controlling his hind end. This happens when you ask him for a turn on the forehand or a lead departure. If you apply both legs simultaneously in this position, you're asking for impulsion or speed.

For the best application of leg cues, think of a phased approach of *ask, insist*, and *demand*. When cueing to any of the three zones, *ask* first by pressing with your lower calf. If your horse doesn't respond, *insist* by bumping with your calf. If he still doesn't respond, *demand* with pressure from your spur. If you still don't get the response you're after, roll your spur in the same area as you've been pressing and bumping (figs. 4.6 A–C).

To develop lightness in your horse, always strive to get the response you desire from the lightest cue possible—in other words, don't bring out your "bigger guns" until you need them.

▸ Develop a catchphrase to use whenever the situation gets frustrating. When you feel your emotion rising (such as when your horse just isn't "getting it"), say to yourself, "Easy, try again," or "Wow—I sure didn't explain that very well," or "Remember—I'm the teacher." Above all, keep your temper in check and stay on track. I tell riders to pretend their horse is a foreign exchange student who doesn't speak the same language—so insisting and getting angry is going to do absolutely no good.

▸ To check your position, have someone watch you and comment from the ground, or take a series of photos or a video of you riding.

▸ Ask an experienced horseman to "be the horse" at the bit end of your reins, to help you learn how to influence your horse's mouth and feel what's going on. He can react to your cues the way a horse would, as well as present various scenarios to test your ability to "talk back."

▸ To improve your balance and leg position, ride bareback or just drop your stirrups. Even better, have an experienced friend longe your horse while you ride him without reins, concentrating on balance and relaxation. When you get really good at that, close your eyes as you trot and lope.

▸ Practice "belly breathing" as you ride, drawing each breath deep into your abdomen and coordinating your breaths to your horse's strides. Experiment with using your breath to influence your horse, for example, "exhaling" him to a stop from the walk, trot, and lope.

# 5 | THE SEVEN ESSENTIALS

There are a few basics every horse should be able to do before going on to specialize in any discipline. These are what we "put on" a colt in the first 60 to 90 days of his training; they're also what we use to tune up an older horse or "fix" a problem horse.

If reining is your goal, these basics are especially critical, as they form the foundation for all reining maneuvers. They're also what we come back to whenever more advanced maneuvers start to fall apart.

I call them the Seven Essentials. They are:

**1** Giving the Face (p. 41)

**2** Walking a Perfect Circle (p. 47)

**3** Walking a Counter-Arc Circle (p. 52)

**4** Backing-Up (p. 54)

**5** Responding to "Whoa" (p. 56)

**6** Moving Off Your Leg (p. 59)

**7** Pivoting On the Hind End (p. 64)

They sound straightforward, and in many ways they are. But teaching them well is a challenge. For exam-ple, almost anyone can get a horse to walk in a circle. But to get him to walk a correct circle, at a consistent pace and with a proper bend, with hind feet following directly in the steps of the front, and with no attention paid to enticing magnets (see p. 19)—that takes skill only attained with know-how, patience, and the time necessary.

I'm going to give you the know-how in this chap-ter. If you have the patience, you'll devote the neces-sary time, and eventually you'll develop the skill. My philosophy of progress by tiny increments—remem-ber, as little as 1 percent a day—is critical here. Extra time spent nailing these basics will pay you terrific divi-dends as you move forward. So, go slow, tackle them in this order, and take the time it takes to get them right.

## Essential 1: Giving the Face

"Giving the face" is all about flexion—vertically and lat-erally. You want the horse to soften in the jaw and flex willingly at the poll in response to light pressure on both reins, or flex to the left or right in response to left- or right-rein pressure. It's also called "coming soft to the pull," and it's the single most important thing to teach your horse.

Why? Because it's how you and your horse both know that you are in control. By softening through the jaw and flexing at the poll, your horse says, "I'm yours. What do you want me to do?" On the other hand, if he even thinks that "putting his head on upside down" (i.e., lifting his head and bracing with his neck) is an option, then you don't have control of his mind or his body. That can be downright scary on a 1,000-pound animal!

Getting a horse to flex at the poll and soften in the jaw is relatively easy, but keeping him that way at all speeds, through transitions, and in all maneuvers—now that is a lifelong endeavor.

It's worth the effort. Just as the Seven Essentials are the key to all reining maneuvers, "giving the face" is the key to the other six Essentials. That's why it's where we begin. I'll start by describing exactly what you're striving for.

### The Goal

Ultimately, your horse should stay soft and flexed in response to your picking up the rein, so that his face is essentially at or slightly behind the vertical, or more or less perpendicular to the ground. He shouldn't be so flexed that his face comes far behind the vertical with his chin tucking toward his chest.

As he gets better at flexing and dropping his head, he should also soften in the jaw, which means his mouth will feel soft—not braced or pulling—on your hand. As he softens to you, his face should always be slightly behind the vertical. Ideally, he'll remain soft even with a little slack in the reins.

If you ask him the way I'm going to describe—using your legs to keep his hind end engaged—he should over time begin to round his topline, too, reaching far up underneath himself with his hind legs (what I call "shortening the wheelbase"). He should stay relaxed, rather than getting agitated. Eventually you'll feel him getting better balanced under you.

**5.1** "Giving the face" from the ground

**To ask your horse to "give his face" from the ground, stand next to his head (not in front of him) and grasp the reins just behind the bit, applying gentle backward pressure. The instant he responds by bringing his nose back and down, as my mare is here, release the pressure and praise him.**

### Here's How

#### From the Ground

Outfit your horse with a snaffle bit and saddle, then stand facing him, just off to one side so you're not directly in front. Grasp a rein just behind the bit with each hand, and apply gentle backward pressure (fig. 5.1). If need be, slide the bit gently from side to side (but avoid a harsh "see-sawing" effect). The instant your horse responds by bringing his nose back or down—"gives"—release the pressure and praise him. Note: it's more important to get him to respond willingly several times than to hold him longer in the flexion.

## It Ain't So

**MYTH: Pulling on your horse makes him hard-mouthed.**

Not necessarily. It depends on when and how you pull and, even more importantly, when you release. A horse must learn to "take a pull" in order to be trained. It won't make his mouth hard *if* you do it correctly: you pull at the right time (without jerking), and you release the instant he responds. I don't think a horse can become soft in the bridle without having been pulled on (the correct way) to some extent. Remember: it's not the *pulling* that educates your horse; it's the *properly timed release*.

Timing is critically important. Remember, your horse learns from the release of pressure (the reward), not the application of it (the pull). Also, he assumes what he was doing immediately before the release is what he's being rewarded for. So to reiterate: reward that very first "give," by releasing pressure and praising him the instant you feel him respond.

Continue asking, and try to get a little more vertical flexion as your horse begins to understand the drill.

Once he's responding well, reposition yourself so you're facing the saddle on the near (left) side. Grasp the near rein, and draw it back and up, in a pull-and-release fashion, toward the saddle horn (to approximate the angle of your pull when you're mounted). When your horse's head is partway around, hold the rein still and wait for him to "give" that last little bit on his own. The instant he does, drop the rein, releasing all pressure, and praise him. Repeat, trying for a more willing response and a bit more lateral bend as he comes to understand what you want. Then move to the other side and flex him similarly in that direction.

Repeat these flexing exercises before every riding session for a while.

### At a Standstill

After your horse is flexing well, both vertically and laterally, from the ground, mount and ask him to flex at a standstill. Take the same approach: that is, with your hands about 12 to 24 inches apart, first draw back gently but firmly with both reins, moving the bit from side to side slightly if need be to get your horse to flex at the poll, drop his head, and soften. Release pressure and praise him the instant he responds (make sure he's actually "giving" to you—softening to your hand—and not just dropping his head), then repeat.

To ask for lateral flexion, slide one hand halfway down the corresponding rein, then draw that hand back toward your waist. The key here is to pull and release: try to get your horse to volunteer that last little bit of bend to the side, then pitch the rein loose and praise him. Repeat several times, then do the same exercise with the other rein.

Repeat these flexing exercises each time you mount and before you begin your riding session.

### At a Walk, Trot, Lope

When he's becoming solid in his flexing at a standstill,

5.2 "Giving the face" from the saddle

**To ask your horse to "give his face" from the saddle, set your hands and bump with both legs in neutral position to bring his face to the vertical. When he softens to your hand as is shown here—note the slack in the rein—his face may come slightly behind the vertical.**

## It Ain't So

MYTH: Riding with low hands encourages your horse to lower his head.

No, it doesn't. Remember, your hands and forearms should always be part of a straight line that runs from your elbows to the bit (see p. 37). Pulling down on your reins—thus breaking that straight line—just gives your horse better leverage to stick his head up and brace against you. If you keep your hands slightly above the swells of your saddle, you'll be able to effectively influence your horse and maintain control. I can't think of any time when it would be advantageous to pull them down below your thighs.

Start on a straight line. Walk him forward, and as you ask him to flex vertically by exerting pressure on both reins (just as you did at the standstill and from the ground), keep your lower legs on in neutral position with as much pressure as necessary to keep him moving forward at the same pace.

As you ask for lateral flexion, move him onto a small circle (about 20 feet in diameter), using your inside leg in neutral position to encourage him to bend through his body as your direct rein asks him to flex his neck to the inside. The bend in his neck should enable you to see just the corner of his eye.

When he's responding well at a walk, try it at a trot, and then a lope, using the same approach (you'll need slightly larger circles at the faster gaits). Remember—you're using your legs to create impulsion up into the bridle (figs. 5.3 A–D).

try it at a walk, but with one key difference: in motion, always use your legs in concert with your hands (fig. 5.2). This keeps him moving forward (rather than just slowing down), eventually, encouraging his hind legs to reach well up underneath him.

**5.3 A–D** "Giving the face" at the trot and lope

At the trot, remember to use your legs in neutral position to create impulsion up into the bridle. This young mare is moving nicely forward, but in A, I'm not yet asking her to "give her face." In B, I'm beginning to ask, and she's beginning to give just a little, and in C, she's beginning to get the idea. Note how she's maintaining slight flexion at the poll ("giving her face") on a soft rein. At the lope, as at the trot, be sure to create impulsion with your legs. As I drive with my legs and create a "wall" with my hands in D, my mare is showing nice vertical flexion at the poll, rounding through her back, and reaching well underneath herself with her hind legs.

"Doubling" and Circling are important safety measures. They're a way of regaining control of your horse when he gets strong or excited. By actively directing the movement of his feet, you keep him from his own, wayward maneuvers, plus reestablish that you are in control, not he.

Once you've got your horse consistently "giving his face," both vertically and laterally to each side, you can begin Doubling him on the fence—that is, turning him abruptly into the fence so that he goes around 180 degrees in his tracks, ending up pointed in the opposite direction from which he was traveling. You can also "chase" him around in a small circle, keeping his neck bent and his feet moving freely and evenly. The circle is simply 360 degrees in either direction—toward or away from the fence. In both Doubling and Circling, the fence provides a barrier that helps solidify or regain control of a situation.

Doubling also serves to recapture your horse's attention when he's ignoring you, and Circling helps to soften your horse when he's stiff and resisting your cues.

### Here's How
#### Doubling
Ride at a trot down the long side of your arena, let's say counterclockwise. Shorten your reins as necessary so that you can use them at need without jerking.

Sit down deep in your saddle, without leaning back. Draw back on your right rein (outside, in this instance) so that your hand moves toward your right-side belt loop. As you draw with that rein, keep a steadying pressure on your left rein (inside) while still allowing your horse's head to come around to the right. Apply pressure with your left leg at the cinch or directly behind it as soon as your horse is committed to the turn and pull him around on his hind end.

Once your horse is facing the opposite direction, trot off again immediately, then repeat the maneuver, turning into the fence the other way. Practice at a trot until he's fluid at it; then teach it at a lope.

#### Circling
To circle him (any time he's getting out of control, ignoring you, or getting stiff), simply extend the Doubling—using the scenario above, keep pulling him around in the same direction, but this time using your right leg (or, if need be, swatting him softly on his right flank with the ends of your reins), so that he turns 380 degrees with all four feet moving evenly (this is not a spin, a pivot, or a cartwheel). Note: This is also not the "perfect circle" you learn in Essential 2 (see p.47)! This is a corrective measure.

Keep Circling until he "comes soft"—that is, he stops pulling back against your hand or resisting in any way, and he feels balanced. Then sit quietly for a moment before resuming work.

Be sure to "visit both sides," so that you're not always Circling in the same direction.

### Putting It All Together
Here's an exercise that combines the flexing lessons using transitions: practice getting and keeping flexion going from a trot to a lope to a trot, then down to a walk for a step or two, then stop and back up. Strive for softness in these transitions—especially the downward ones from a lope to a trot and a trot to a walk. Mix them up and do a lot of them!

☞ *Troubleshoot It*

When the horse:

Overbridles (brings the chin too close to the chest—fig. 5.4): Use more leg and less rein, being sure to release when your horse softens. If need be use distinct tugs to make it uncomfortable when he puts his head beyond the vertical or too low, returning to soft hands as soon as he corrects his positioning.

Underbridles (doesn't flex enough; neck may be raised and braced against your hands): Bump incrementally harder with your legs in neutral position (see p. 39) or just behind it while holding with your hands as assertively as need be until there is the slightest indication of the horse "giving," then release immediately. Repeat.

Never fully softens the jaw (pulls on you even though he's flexed at the poll and dropped his head): Tug on the reins alternately off the beat of his motion. Be sure not to tug predictably, or he may simply learn to move his head from side to side without truly softening and giving. Also, make sure the slack is out of the reins before you tug, so you're not jerking on the bit.

"Wiggles" (his rear end drifts off to one side or the other instead of driving up underneath his body): Ride assertively, bumping simultaneously with both legs in neutral position or just behind it. Push him up into the "wall" of your hands to straighten him out.

## Essential 2: Walking a Perfect Circle

When your horse is responding well to Essential 1: Giving His Face, begin work on Essential 2: Walking a Perfect Circle. This one sounds easy, but it isn't! Once you achieve it, though, you'll understand the basics of maintaining control over your horse's entire body—a must for reining. Plus, this circle will serve as the foundation for the circles and spins you'll see in all the patterns to come.

**5.4** "Overbridled"

**If your hands keep pulling when your horse "gives" to you, or if you fail to use enough leg, he'll come too far behind the vertical, like this.**

When riding your perfect circles, you'll also discover and need to overcome your horse's magnets—distractions (the barn, the trailer, or his buddies) that attract him and threaten to destroy the geometry of his circle.

### The Goal

A perfect circle is a symmetric circle, meaning precisely round—not oval, oblong, or egg-shaped! As your horse travels this circle, he should stay soft in your hand and be flexed slightly to the inside through his neck and body. He should walk in an even, four-beat rhythm, at a steady pace with no deviations in speed. His hind feet should follow in the tracks of his front. He should be equally soft and responsive in either direction.

Here's a tip: work on freshly raked ground so you can easily see your horse's tracks, and enlist a friend to help you gauge the symmetry of your circles.

### Here's How

Walk your horse forward, using both your legs in neu-

## It Ain't So

MYTH: Every horse has his "good" and "bad" side.

It's not a question of good and bad; it's a question of hollow and stiff. Most (but not all) horses are asymmetrical in a way that makes it easier for them to bend excessively going to the right (their hollow side) and harder for them to bend going to the left (their stiff side). When riders think in terms of good and bad, they naturally assume they should work the bad side more to bring it up to the level of the good.

But the so-called good side—in reality, the hollow side—needs as much work as the so-called bad or stiff side, or else it can become just as problematic (because of the tendency to bend excessively on the hollow side while dropping the shoulder on the stiff side). So work both your horse's sides equally, giving intelligent consideration to the tendencies of each side and how to compensate for them.

**5.5** The circle

**To walk a correct circle, bump with both legs in neutral position to move your horse forward in an energetic rhythm, then apply light pressure to your inside (direct) rein, tipping his nose to the inside. Encourage him to bend onto the arc of the circle with pressure from your inside leg (here, my left leg) in neutral position.**

corner of his inside eye) and begin the circle (fig. 5.5). Use leg pressure and your outside rein as need be to keep the circle round—more on that in a moment. As I explained in the Working Vocabulary (p. 15), most horses tend to be asymmetrical; going to their "hollow" (usually right) side, they tend to bend too much. Going to their "stiff" (often left) side, they tend to resist bending. You'll need to compensate for this.

### Dealing with the Hollow Side

When circling to the right, your horse may tend to tip his nose in more easily and bend too much, cocking his rear end into the circle while the circle gradually enlarges due to his position and centrifugal force (fig. 5.6).

To correct this, apply your inside (right) leg behind neutral position to push his rear end back out onto the track of the circle. At the same time, keep enough tension on the outside (left) rein to keep his shoulder from

tral position to move him in an energetic rhythm. Keeping both your legs active, and with your hands 12 to 24 inches apart, apply light, direct-rein pressure on what will become the inside rein to tip his nose to the inside of the circle (so that you can just see the

**5.6** Correcting problems on the right-hand circle

Because of their natural asymmetry, when circling to the right many horses tend to tip their nose in (more easily than when going left), bend too much, and cock their rear end to the inside. This position and centrifugal force then cause the circle to gradually enlarge. (Note: though I find this scenario to be the most prevalent by far, some horses' asymmetry is opposite.) To correct, apply your inside (right) leg behind neutral position to push the horse's rear end back out. Keep enough tension on the outside (indirect) rein to keep his shoulder from drifting out to the left, straightening out his neck a bit so you can just see the corner of his right eye. Apply your left leg at the cinch; that will also help to keep that shoulder from drifting.

drifting out to the left, straightening out his neck a bit so you can just see the corner of his right eye. Apply your left leg at the cinch to help keep that shoulder from drifting out.

### Dealing with the Stiff Side

Circling to the left, your horse may tend to resist bending, keeping his body relatively straight while refusing to bring his nose to the inside (fig. 5.7). Instead, he leads with his inside (left) shoulder, letting his hind end drift out while the forehand somewhat collapses the circle.

**5.7** Correcting problems on the left-hand circle

Circling to the left, your horse may tend to resist bending or bringing his nose to the inside, instead leading with his inside (left) shoulder and letting his hind end drift out. To correct, pick up his inside shoulder with a "key in the ignition" lift and twist (see fig. 5.8 A). Also apply pressure with your inside (left) leg in neutral position to encourage more bend, while pulling your outside (indirect) rein slightly outward to the right, thus moving his shoulders out to the right. If necessary, use your right leg a few inches behind neutral position to keep his hindquarters from moving out.

To correct this, pick up his inside shoulder with a move I call "key in the ignition" (figs. 5.8 A & B). Bring your inside (left) rein hand close to his neck, then twist your wrist as if you're turning a key in a car ignition, so that your palm comes to face upward, making your pinkie finger closest to the neck (while keeping that rein on that side of the neck—do not bring your hand over the neck or withers, a common error). This tightens the rein slightly while giving a "lifting" motion that helps raise the shoulder on that side.

At the same time, apply pressure with your inside

**5.8 A & B** The "key in the ignition"
In A you can see me performing the "key in the ignition" correction when circling to the left: I twist and lift my inside (left) hand to "palm-up" position while keeping it close to the horse's neck in order to "pick up" the horse's inside shoulder. In B I'm lifting my horse's right shoulder on a circle to the right with a "key in the ignition" lift of the inside (direct) rein, with supporting pressure from my outside (indirect) rein.

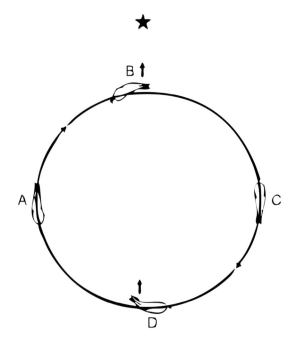

(left) leg in neutral position (that is, directly behind the cinch) to encourage more bend, while pulling your outside (indirect) rein slightly outward to the right, moving his shoulders out to the right to help stop the forehand from collapsing in on the circle. If necessary, use your right leg a few inches behind neutral position to keep his hindquarters from moving out.

As you strive to keep him aligned on the arc of the circle in either direction, remember to keep him "giving his face" (that is, staying soft to your hand) and use both your legs to keep him moving forward at a steady pace.

**5.9** Dealing with magnets
The star represents a "magnet" (the barn, arena gate, trailer, pasture buddies) that's attracting your horse. At A and C, your horse may travel correctly on the line of the circle. But at B the magnet tends to pull his shoulders *out of* the circle, and at D it tends to pull his shoulders *into* the circle. You must correct for this to keep your circles perfectly round (see text).

**5.10** Correcting leaning in

When a horse leans in on the circle, pick up his inside shoulder with a "key in the ignition" move with your inside (direct) rein (see fig. 5.8 A). At the same time, bring your outside (indirect) rein away from his neck and use your inside leg at the cinch to bring his shoulders back onto the circle, as I am doing here.

**5.11** Correcting drifting out

My horse is trying to drift to his right out of the circle, toward a magnet that's attracting him. To correct this, I'm using pressure from my outside (indirect) rein against my horse's neck and my outside leg (here, my right) at or just behind the cinch to stop the drift of his outside shoulder. Meanwhile, my inside (direct) rein continues to guide his nose to the inside of the circle.

### ☞ Troubleshoot It

When the horse:

Falls in toward a "magnet": You're on the side of the circle that's farthest from the barn, and your horse speeds up and cuts in on the circle because he wants to go to the barn (a magnet—fig. 5.9). Pick up the shoulder that's falling in, using the key in the ignition movement I described on p. 49. At the same time, pull your outside rein away from the barn and use your inside leg at the cinch to push his shoulders outward onto the circle (fig. 5.10). Then overcorrect slightly by making your horse move a bit farther out on the far side of the circle, while still maintaining his body on the same arc. (An overcor-

rection works because it eventually enables the two of you to "meet" in the middle—correct—ground.)

Bows out toward a "magnet": You're on the side of the circle closest to the barn this time (see fig. 5.9). Your horse pulls or drifts toward the barn, bulging the circle out in that direction. Draw your outside rein back and against your horse's neck, to stop the outward drift of his shoulder, and apply your outside leg in neutral position to correct the outward bulge in his barrel (fig. 5.11). Overcorrect slightly by making him cut across circle (as if, on a baseball diamond, you're going from first base to third, and leaving out "second").

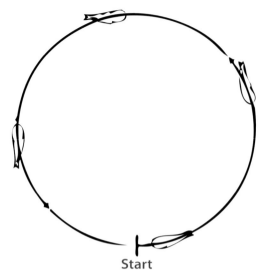

**Start**

5.12 The counter-arc circle

Riding a counter-arc circle is a bit like sidepassing on a circle. **Your horse's nose tips to the outside while his front legs cross over each other on a slightly larger circle than the one his hind legs make. To ride a counter-arc circle to the left, apply light pressure on your right (indirect) rein to tip your horse's nose to the outside. At the same time, open your left (direct) rein slightly away from your horse's neck, to indicate leftward movement, and apply clear pressure with your right leg in neutral position or a bit behind to keep his hindquarters on a slightly smaller circle than his forehand.**

Loses impulsion and focus ("wandering"): Drive vigorously with both legs in neutral position and cluck to keep him motivated and moving with energy.

## Essential 3: Walking a Counter-Arc Circle

For this exercise, your horse moves in a circle, but with his nose tipped to the outside. His front legs, meanwhile, cross over each other, making a slightly larger circle than his hind legs—sort of like sidepassing on a circle (fig. 5.12). It's a challenging exercise but definitely worth the time and effort to master, as it will help you start to gain control of your horse's shoulders. This, in turn, gives you the ammunition you'll need, much later, to correct a spin in which your horse's shoulders quit "driving." (Note: though we commonly use this term in

association with the horse's hindquarters and forward movement, in a spin, the hind end remains static while the shoulders move—or drive—the body energetically around it.)

Walking in a counter-arc circle also refines your control over your horse's head, neck, and shoulders, and increases your overall awareness of how your rein and leg cues influence your horse's body.

### The Goal

Like the circle in Essential 2, this one should be perfectly round with one exception: instead of the hind feet following directly in the tracks of the front, the front feet are on a slightly larger circle than the hind. Because it involves lateral as well as forward movement, your horse's front legs should be slightly, but evenly crossing over each other.

Your horse should also stay soft in your hand, his shoulders driving with cadence.

### Here's How

I'll describe a counter-arc circle to the left (to do one to the right, simply reverse all cues). Walk your horse forward, using both your legs in neutral position to move him in an energetic rhythm. Apply light pressure to your right (indirect) rein to tip your horse's nose to the outside (so that you can just see the corner of his left eye). At the same time, open your left (direct) rein slightly away from your horse's neck, to indicate leftward movement, and apply clear pressure with your right leg in neutral position or a bit behind (figs. 5.13 A–C). Remember—you want his hindquarters to be on a slightly smaller circle than his forehand.

If your horse doesn't respond, use your cues more actively. Once he begins to respond, continue to cue him rhythmically to encourage him to move smoothly and with cadence around the circle. Keep a feeling contact with the right rein to keep his jaw soft and his nose tipped to the outside.

**5.13 A–C** Cues for the counter-arc circle

Walking a counter-arc circle refines control of your horse's head, neck, and shoulders while increasing your overall awareness of how your rein and leg cues influence your horse's body. Circle to the left, using both legs to urge your horse forward in an energetic rhythm; then apply light pressure to your right (indirect) rein to tip your horse's nose to the outside, and open your left (direct) rein slightly away from your horse's neck (A). This use of your reins keeps your horse's neck flexed to the right as he moves in a circle to the left (B). To encourage the counter-bend throughout his body apply clear pressure with your right leg in neutral position (C).

Note, this is a challenging exercise, so here's a tip: before you attempt to ride it, try it on foot, without your horse. Draw a 20-foot-diameter circle in the dirt, then move yourself laterally around it, tipping your head to the outside and imagining that your legs are your horse's front legs as they step sideways over each other. Think and feel how you need to influence your horse's body with your hands and legs to accomplish the same circle mounted.

When you do attempt it mounted, give your horse (and yourself) time to figure it out. Be patient and pay close attention to how your cues influence your horse, and you'll find your "feel" in the saddle increasing dramatically.

### ☞ Troubleshoot It

Your horse's response will be affected by his natural asymmetry (his stiff and hollow sides) as well as by whatever magnets are drawing his attention at any moment. As when riding a regular circle, use the "key in the ignition" movement to correct falling in, and your leg at or behind neutral position as need be to adjust the position of his hindquarters.

## Essential 4: Backing-Up

Backing-up is important because it's not only a maneuver in itself, but also the correction for a poor stop. At this point, however, backing-up doesn't mean the same as it will later on (when you'll want it "super straight," very fast, and in response to few visible cues). For now, you just want to introduce the concept clearly, calmly, and patiently. The worst thing you can do right now is to try to go fast and sacrifice correctness and softness.

### The Goal

Your horse will maintain a soft face (that is, he won't brace against the bit) as he takes a few willing steps backward, reasonably straight.

### Here's How

#### From the Ground

With your horse in a snaffle bit and saddle, stand facing him, just off to one side so you're not directly in front. Grasp both reins just behind the bit—one in each hand—and apply gentle backward pressure as you did to ask him to bring his nose back and down in the face-softening exercise (see p. 42). If necessary, slide the bit gently from side to side while maintaining soft pressure on both reins.

When he responds by dropping his nose down and back, don't release the pressure as you did for face softening. Instead, maintain a gentle, intermittent pressure and cluck. If he hesitates, be patient. It's better to wait him out (he'll give in eventually) than to start applying more and more pressure. Most horses are willing to do this for us if we're patient and ask for just a step or two at a time in the beginning (figs. 5.14 A & B).

The moment he takes a single backward step, release all pressure and praise him with hands and voice. Then repeat, over time asking for two backward steps, then three. At this point, don't worry about whether he's perfectly straight as he backs up. You're just looking for willing compliance. (Remember from chapter 2 that key concept of setting your horse up to succeed by *showing him* until he understands and accepts, and then training him how you want him to do it—in this case, to back up straight—and only then asking for speed. It's especially important here.)

#### While Mounted

From his back, use the same rein action you used successfully from the ground. Apply your legs at the same time, bumping your horse's sides gently from neutral position, with increasing pressure as necessary to gain response, but not so much that he wants to move forward "through" the bit (fig. 5.15).

Again, ask for just one step at a time. The moment he complies, release all rein and leg pressure and praise

**5.14 A & B** The backup from the ground
Begin teaching your horse a correct backup from the ground. Stand facing him, just off to the side. Grasp the reins just behind the bit and apply gentle backward pressure, asking him to bring his nose back and down just as you did in the "give the face" exercise. But when he drops his head, keep the pressure on to ask for one backward step, then stop and praise him. If he needs extra help understanding that you want him to back up, place one hand on his face, as I am in B, and push gently back.

him lavishly. Gradually ask for more steps, without worrying at this point whether he's straight.

Once he willingly moves back three or four steps, begin asking for straightness, as well. Because of natural asymmetry, most horses will tend to back with their rear end veering to the right. To prevent this, apply pressure with your right leg a few inches behind

**5.15** The backup from the saddle
When mounted, use the same rein action you used successfully from the ground to ask for a backup. At the same time, bump gently with your legs in neutral position. Again, ask for just one step at a time. Except for the slight opening of his mouth, I like how my horse is backing here—soft, flexed, and one step at a time.

neutral position to push his hindquarters back to the left, using your right rein as necessary to help align him. (Eventually, you'll correct this by moving his shoulders to the right, instead, but that requires more shoulder control than we have at this point.)

### ☞ Troubleshoot It

When the horse:

Braces against the bit: Ask him to soften by bumping the bit gently side to side while also bumping his sides with your legs to get him to release. When he softens his jaw, release the bit pressure for an instant, then cluck or bump a bit more to get him to step back. Then release completely, let him stand a moment, and ask for more softening and backing-up.

Backs up crookedly: Stop asking for backward movement and instead use your leg behind neutral position as appropriate (right leg for a rightward drift; left leg for a leftward drift) to push his hind end back in line. Then resume backing, keeping that same leg on him as need be to encourage straightness.

Wants to rear instead: This results from confusion— your horse can't figure out that he must move his feet in response to a pull on his face. In this event, don't change your aids, but be even more patient. In other words, keep your hands and legs as they were just before your horse began threatening to rear, and patiently wait him out. The instant he steps back, release and reward.

If need be, dismount and review the backup cue from the ground. Then stand next to the saddle, with both reins going around the right side of the saddle horn. Pull softly and intermittently on both reins, simulating the action of your hands when you're mounted. Once he backs up, mount and try again. Never risk having your horse actually rear while you're mounted; the worst wreck you can have is a horse falling over

on you. Work from the ground as need be to avoid it, and if you continue to have difficulty with this, seek professional help.

Quits (he decides he's backed far enough): The best cure for this is prevention—in other words, try to stop asking for the backup before your horse wants to quit (yet another reason to proceed slowly and deliberately). If it happens anyway, ask for just one more step backward, then release your aids, praise him, sit quietly for a moment, and then ask one more time with a goal of getting a few willing steps. If you abandon the lesson instead, you're letting your horse train you. This is one of the first places a horse will really test you, so be patient and calm, but be sure you win.

## Essential 5: Responding to "Whoa"

Your horse's willingness to stop when you say "Whoa" is essential for control and basic training. It also provides the foundation for one of reining's most thrilling maneuvers, the sliding stop. Here, you'll be satisfied by an attempt at ceasing forward motion. It's not going to look anything like the stop we'll need in competition, where the horse is balanced, "off" the bit (not leaning on it), driving from behind with his back round and his head low, gliding into the dirt. I get goose bumps just thinking about it!

But all things in good time. The key thing now is to get your horse to love, even crave stopping (i.e., "hunt the stop"). That means don't make it uncomfortable for him. Make it as easy as possible. Set him up for success by making sure he's a little tired and already wanting to stop, then aim him toward a wall or a corner if need be so he has a visual barrier. Next exhale and say "Whoa," get him to stop, and praise him. This is much preferable to trying to force him to stop by over-pulling on the reins, which he doesn't understand yet anyway.

If you do it right, you'll be surprised how quickly your horse will learn to stop when he hears "Whoa." In fact, he may start to stop when he feels you begin to exhale!

### The Goal

When you sit deep, exhale, and say "Whoa," your horse will come to a comfortable stop on his rear end, then back up a step, all preferably without your having to pull on the reins (although you probably will need to pull in the beginning, as you'll see).

### Here's How

Prepare to make stopping your horse's idea (remember, make the right thing easy!) by loping him until he's a bit tired and probably thinking about stopping. As you lope, work on getting him soft in the face by using both your legs in neutral position to drive him into your hands. Work on circles, asking him to bend by using pressure or bumping from your inside leg in neutral position.

When he's ready to volunteer to slow down (you know because you have to push to keep him loping), ride him onto a straight line toward your arena wall or a corner (fig. 5.16). You're going to ask for the stop when you're about three or four strides from the wall or corner, so give yourself enough space to be able to straighten him out before you get to that point.

You needn't worry about exactly where his feet are; if you exhale as I describe, then say "Whoa," you'll be asking in the right part of his stride to make it work.

When you're about three or four strides from the wall or corner, just when he's starting to wonder which

**5.16** Using the corner to stop

**Make stopping easy and comfortable for your horse. After loping him to tire him enough so that he *wants* to stop, aim him toward a wall or a corner—a visual barrier to help him stop.**

way you're going to go, take a long breath, exhale as you sit deep in the saddle, and at the end of the exhalation, say "Whoa" in a low, smooth, authoritative voice. (If your voice is tentative, abrupt, or too drawn-out, it will be less effective at commanding attention and getting a response.)

As you finish saying "Whoa," in the same breath say "One, and," and if he hasn't stopped by then, pick up the reins and, using the least amount of pressure that's effective, get him to stop. Back him up a step, then relax and praise him as you allow him to stand and rest a bit (figs. 5.17 A–C).

**5.17 A–C** Stopping soft

**To ask for the stop, take a deep breath, then exhale as you sit deep in the saddle (A). At the end of the exhalation, say "Whoa," in a low, smooth, authoritative voice, reinforcing the command with light rein pressure as necessary while remaining upright without leaning or slumping, and maintaining the line from your horse's mouth, through your hand, to your elbow (B). My horse is stopping "soft," nicely balanced on his hind end (C).**

Keep in mind that it's okay to pull on him a little to get him to stop as long as you always give him a chance to stop before you pull. If you pull at the same time as you say "Whoa," he'll never learn to stop just from your voice. (Plus, it can cause him to stop abruptly and unbalanced, "dashboarding" you, his driver.)

Be sure to give him a long enough break after the stop so that he knows he's being rewarded. Watch to see that he relaxes (drops his head, exhales) and licks his lips—a sign that he's "processing" and is fine with the new information he's just been given.

Above all, don't let your horse call the shots on where to stop. This can happen without you realizing it: don't let him "volunteer" to stop at his preferred spots, such as by the out gate or near other horses, and don't avoid stopping in places where he doesn't want to stop or is drawn forward by magnets. Insist that he stop at the places you've chosen, and correct him as I describe in the troubleshooting section, below.

Otherwise, you're letting him train you.

### ☞ Troubleshoot It

When the horse:

Doesn't stop: Use the Doubling and Circling maneuvers I described earlier in this chapter (see p. 46). Both Doubling and Circling will feel a lot like work to your horse, so he'll learn that simply stopping is a lot easier. Once his feet stop moving, release all aids and sit while you praise him.

Stops reluctantly: Get his attention by being a bit more

assertive with your hands as you're backing him a step or two once he does stop. Then sit for a while and make a big fuss over what a good boy he is.

Stops on his front end (he'll feel as if he's propping himself with his front legs): Shift his center of gravity back by sitting back yourself and picking up your reins about as high as your lower rib cage (don't pull down toward your hips) and holding them steady while you bump with your legs in neutral position until your horse backs up and gets "off" the bit. It will feel as though his shoulders have lifted up into the area under the front of the saddle and his back has rounded. Then, the next time you ask for the stop, make sure you're driving him with your legs to keep his hind end engaged as he stops and then backs up off the bit.

Stops crookedly (by leaning or dropping a shoulder): I'll have a lot more to say about this later (see p. 94), but for now notice that your horse probably leans to his left side (because of that natural asymmetry) or toward the magnet of the barn or the out gate.

First, don't ask for the stop if your horse is moving crookedly—go around again and use your reins and legs to straighten him out, and then ask. If, despite your best effort, he's still not straight when he stops, back him up a few steps on the straight line you were originally on, then turn him 180 degrees away from the barn (or whatever the magnet was). For example, if he's leaning left and you're correcting him to the right, bring your right rein back toward your right outside belt loop and let your left hand come toward that same belt loop, only stopping at his neck (without crossing over it) as you push him with your left leg at the cinch and roll him back to the right.

## Essential 6: Moving Off Your Leg

Getting your horse to move off your leg—moving laterally—is key to getting total control of his body. Lateral control of the hind end and shoulders helps you with simple moves, like opening and closing gates or backing in a straight line. It also makes possible more advanced maneuvers, like changing leads and spinning.

Horses naturally move *into* pressure, so young or green horses must be educated to move *away* from it, instead.

Ultimately, lateral control will enable you to "leg-yield" your horse diagonally across the arena at a lope—resistance-free, body straight, front legs crossing over each other. It will also help you execute a perfect sidepass, such as moving sideways down the length of a log, as seen in a trail class.

For now, however, you should be satisfied with any movement sideways in response to leg pressure; the more refined lateral control will come later. In these exercises, you ask your horse to move his rear end over as you stand next to him (at the hitching rack and then as you hold the reins), and while you're mounted (maneuvering him next to a gate to open it, sideways along the fence line, and finally diagonally across the arena).

### The Goal

Your horse will maintain a soft face (i.e., he won't brace against the bit) as he, first, willingly moves his rear end a few steps sideways in response to pressure, and second, willingly moves his front end (the shoulders) a few steps sideways in response to pressure. You work toward getting both ends to move together, for a "whole-body" move to the side.

In the movement at the gate and along the fence line, and in the more advanced maneuver diagonally across the arena (the leg-yield), at first he'll move his front end followed by his hind end separately. Eventually, he'll move both ends simultaneously in the leg-yield.

### Here's How
#### At the Hitching Rack
Practice this one whenever you're grooming your

**5.18** Teaching lateral movement with a sweat scraper
**Begin teaching your horse to move his hind end over from the ground. Apply pressure with a sweat scraper or hoof pick about where your heel would be. (I'm a tad high and too far back here, but in the beginning stages you'll probably find this spot works best; then just gradually move closer to where your spur will actually be.) Ask for one lateral step at a time.**

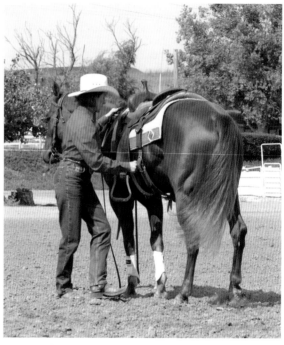

**5.19** Teaching lateral movement with your thumb
**As your horse becomes accustomed to moving away from pressure, you can reinforce the lesson using just your thumb. Remember to work from both sides.**

horse. (Note: if there's any chance your horse will pull back, untie him before conducting this lesson.) Stand at your horse's side, and use a sweat scraper, hoof pick, or other hard object to create pressure (that is, mild discomfort) right where your heel presses on your horse's ribs when you're mounted (fig. 5.18). Your aim is to have him respond to the least amount of pressure possible, so don't start with a jab.

The instant he takes one sideways step with a hind foot, stop and praise him, then ask for another step. If he resists, increase the pressure gradually in a push-and-release movement until he takes at least one step, always looking to get a response from the least amount of pressure, and praising him the instant he reacts. If need be, you can also pull his face toward you slightly as you ask him to move his hindquarters over.

Now go to his other side and ask him to step in the opposite direction, using the same cues. Repeat frequently from both sides until he responds willingly to mild pressure.

### In Hand

With your horse wearing a saddle and bridle, stand next to him, hold the reins in your left hand, and use the sweat scraper, hoof pick, or your thumb to create pressure, again just behind the cinch where your heel would normally be (fig. 5.19). By now, your horse should respond with a sideways step even as you use the reins to keep his head straight. Strive to get him to move just his hind end over.

Switch hands and repeat from the other side.

**5.20** Teaching lateral movement from the saddle
**Another good way to teach lateral movement is with a "prop" that gives a reason for the side-stepping. Use your legs and reins as I describe in the text to move your horse laterally as your friend or assistant opens and closes a gate.**

## Opening a Gate

Now mount up and see if you can move both his front end and his hind end in order to open a gate. Ask a friend to move the gate manually so you have both hands on your reins to influence your horse's body.

Line your horse up parallel to the gate. Have your friend push it open a bit toward you as you ask your horse to step sideways with his front end, away from the gate. You do this by carrying both your hands away from the gate while using the foot that's nearest the gate at the cinch to encourage his shoulders over (fig. 5.20).

After he takes one step with his front end, apply pressure with your "gate-side" heel in the same spot as you did with the sweat scraper to move his hind end over a step, too. If he resists, bump with that heel behind neutral posi-

tion until he takes the step. Go back and forth in this way, moving his front end, then his back end as your friend opens the gate a little at a time. Try to stay parallel to it and move with it until it's open. Then sit there next to it.

Be sure to work in both directions, so your horse is side-stepping both ways. Then try to do it without someone moving the gate for you. Also, reverse all the cues to teach your horse how to close the gate. Take as long as you need to master this step before you move on to work at the fence line.

## At the Fence Line

Still mounted, position your horse so he's facing into, and perpendicular to, a safe fence (nothing he can catch his front feet in or get his head over). First, ask him to move his front end one step to the side, then his hind end, and then his front again, and so on, so that he's moving sideways down the fence.

To ask the front end to move, bring both your reins over in the desired direction while bumping with your "opposite" foot at the cinch. This means that if you're asking for a step to the left, carry your reins to the left while bumping with your right leg just in front of neutral position.

After he's taken one sideways step with his front end, use the same leg to ask his hind end to move, only this time bumping a few inches behind neutral position (fig. 5.21).

Throughout, adjust your reins as necessary to keep your horse's neck straight and roughly perpendicular to the fence. When he can do it moving freely, front end and then hind end, try to move his whole body at the same time. Get this down well before moving to the next exercise.

## Diagonally Across the Arena

Starting in one corner of your arena, ask your horse to walk forward and sideways diagonally across to the opposite corner, moving first his front end, and then his hind end, then the front again, and so on. Let's say

**5.21** The sidepass

**More lateral work—facing the fence. To sidepass to the left, use your reins to keep your horse perpendicular to the fence, while bumping with your right leg at the cinch to ask the front end to step over, as I am here. Then bump with the same leg behind neutral position to ask the hind end to move over.**

you're in a right-hand corner, and will move him diagonally to the far left-hand corner (figs. 5.22 A–D):

▶ Squeeze with both legs in neutral position to send him forward, then in order to move his front end to the left, bring both reins toward the left and bump with your right leg at the cinch.

▶ Keep forward motion going with a squeeze from both legs, and to move his hind end over, bump with your right leg a few inches behind neutral position.

▶ Repeat the sequence, working your way diagonally across the arena. As your horse comes to understand better what you're asking, work toward getting him to move both ends at the same time in a

true leg-yield. Carry your hands to the left, and use your right leg in neutral position—just behind the cinch.

▶ Reverse all cues and work in the opposite direction. Be sure to provide equal practice going both ways.

When your horse is responding well consistently at the walk, try it at the trot, and eventually the lope.

### ☞ Troubleshoot It

When the horse:

Is uneven (one end—front or hind—gets in front of the other along the fence or diagonally across the arena): Moderate your cues for the end in front and use the cues for the opposite end more strongly. For example, horses usually get their front end ahead of their hind end, so slow the front end down by keeping your hands more neutral and using your outside leg more vigorously behind neutral position to catch the rear end up.

Raises his head/braces his neck: To get him to soften and "drive him up into the bridle," bump with both legs in neutral position for a moment while holding him with both reins. If need be, bump the bit lightly on one side and then the other while you drive with your legs and travel straight ahead for a bit to break up his resistance. Then resume going diagonally.

## Essential 7: Pivoting on the Hind End

The 360-degree pivot on the hind end is the start of what will eventually be your spin, so a correct foundation is extremely important. All major problems in the maneuver, now and later, result from lack of shoulder control. With Essential 3: The Counter-Arc Circle (p. 52) and Essential 6: Moving off the Leg (p. 59), you've started to gain control of your horse's shoulders. With this, the final Essential, you'll build on that control.

A common mistake at this point is to "go faster

**5.22 A–D** Crossing the diagonal with lateral movement

To move your horse forward and laterally across the arena from the right-hand corner to the left-hand corner, carry your hands in the direction of movement and, to move his front end to the left, bump with your right leg at the cinch (A). To move his back end over, bump with your right leg just behind neutral position (B). Ask the front end to move laterally again (C) and then the back end (D). Continue like this, moving forward and laterally, one end at a time, across the arena.

wronger." In other words, eagerness to move a pivot into a spin prompts riders to sacrifice form for speed. Don't do it! Go as slowly as you need to in order to maintain control and do it correctly. In the beginning, think in terms of a 90-degree turn, and then a 180. Build toward the 360 in increments.

There are many different ways of teaching a horse to step his front end around; one tried-and-true method is to walk in your perfect circle, then "tighten it down" while taking care to keep your horse's nose pointed in the direction of the turn. This is the method I'll teach you.

### The Goal

Your horse will make his circle smaller and tighter, while keeping his jaw soft and his neck level, with his nose tipped slightly in the direction of movement. As the circle tightens to a pivot, his outside front leg crosses over the inside one. His hind legs remain more or less in one place (you needn't worry about either of them being "planted"). He moves only as fast as he can while still maintaining proper form.

### Here's How

Begin by reviewing Essential 2: Walking a Perfect Circle (p. 47). Practice in a corner of your arena, so you can use the wall as a visual marker and a physical barrier. As your horse moves forward with energy, use pressure on the inside (direct) rein to keep his nose tipped to the inside (fig. 5.23). Maintain your inside leg in neutral position (to keep the circle round), and support the horse with your outside (indirect) rein against his neck to keep the circle symmetrical.

Gradually begin to reduce the size of the circle. When you're ready to step around, remove the pressure of your inside leg and add a little backward pull on the outside rein by bringing your hand toward your belly button (but not across your horse's neck). Also bump with your outside leg at the cinch.

Remember, your inside rein is to indicate the direction of movement and to keep your horse's nose tipped that way—not to pull your horse around. If you mainly pull that inside rein, you'll pull your horse out of alignment. And, the backward pressure on the outside rein is just to suggest stepping across, and shouldn't be used so much that it pulls your horse's head to the outside, away from the pivot. If you keep him aligned with both reins and both legs, you'll be setting the stage for greater speed later.

In the beginning, don't worry about speed at all—go as slowly as you must in order to keep your horse's body properly aligned, his jaw soft and poll flexed, and his nose correctly tipped. Be satisfied with just a step or two of the front legs crossing over before moving him back onto a slightly larger circle, re-checking proper form. Then try again. Any time he begins to lose that proper form, move immediately onto the larger circle, reestablish his form, then try again.

Gradually, over time, ask your horse to add steps one at a time. If you remain patient and keep showing him how to do it (as opposed to trying to force him), you'll be surprised how quickly he'll be willing to step all the way around. Use your visual marker (the fence, bushes, or other nearby landmarks if you're practicing out on the trail) to keep track of how far around you're going.

Be sure to work equally in both directions. I'll have more to say about the relative challenges of your horse's stiff and hollow sides in chapter 7. For now, concentrate on getting willing steps in each direction.

### ☞ Troubleshoot It

When the horse:

Bends too much: This is caused by the rider trying to pull the horse around with the inside (direct) rein, overbending his neck. It is common to resort to this when you can't make the horse's shoulders move. This actually causes you to end up going in a circle instead of a spin. To correct it, think "kick" more than "pull." Use your legs assertively to keep your horse's body aligned and to keep him moving around; use that inside rein just to keep his nose tipped in the direction of movement.

Counter-bends: This happens when you use too much outside (indirect) rein, trying ineffectually to make the shoulders move, and in the process you pull your horse's head around to the outside and create a counter-bend in his neck. Correct it with your inside rein and a little less outside rein, plus bump with your outside leg at the cinch.

**5.23** The pivot

When you begin a pivot on the hind end, go as slowly as necessary to do it correctly. Here, after walking a smaller and smaller circle to the left, my horse is beginning to step his front end around as I move my outside (indirect) rein toward my belly button and bump with my outside leg at the cinch. Meanwhile, my inside (direct) rein keeps his nose tipped in the direction of movement.

# 6 COLLECTION, STEERING

With the Seven Essentials of the last chapter, you taught your horse the basics he needs in order to progress to this chapter and beyond. You made sure he could do each Essential in turn before you moved on to the next, and you didn't increase speed at backing-up, stopping, or pivoting on the hind end until your horse could do these maneuvers slowly in proper form.

You've accomplished all that, but how can you know if you're truly ready to move on to the collection and steering work in this chapter? Here's how: assess whether you've *internalized* the earlier learning. In other words, you should be able to think of something else, sing a song, or listen to instruction (and actually *hear* it!) while working on any of the Seven Essentials. If you can, that means what you've learned has found its way to the "seat of your pants." You don't have to concentrate so hard to accomplish it; you can *feel* it, instead.

If you've reached that point, you and your horse are ready to move on to developing collection and fine-tuning steering. I'll talk about collection and steering separately, then give you two exercises that are ideal for working on both of these important areas of focus at the same time.

## Collection

Collection, also called getting a horse "framed up," isn't something separate from any other riding goal. It's the way you influence your horse to move *while* doing your turns, circles, spins, and other maneuvers. As your horse moves at any gait, being collected enables him to begin to shift his weight, or center of gravity, to the rear. That's where the engine of this fabulous machine is, so that's where we want most of his weight to be, too. Imagine a front-heavy car with a big, strong motor in the back. The power from behind would drive that front end right into the ground!

As you condense your horse's frame through collection (think of an accordion's movement), it becomes easier for his speed transitions to be smooth (without falling out of the correct lead behind), his spins to be cadenced and "steppy" in front, his stops to glide into the ground. All his maneuvers look precise and polished. It's like the difference between going to the ball in your workboots and going in your dancing shoes!

When your horse is green, his center of gravity is located at about his heart girth, that is, where the cinch goes; this makes him heavy on his front end. His back tends to be hollow (as opposed to rounded the way we want it), causing his hind legs to trail out behind. We call this "strung out."

As he advances in his training and gets better at shifting his weight to the rear, his front end will lighten, enabling you to move his feet via the reins much more efficiently. Collection enables a much clearer, stronger connection from your mind through the reins to your horse's mouth and feet. This is how "lightness" begins.

Collection happens in degrees (figs. 6.1 A–C). Before you start working on "framing your horse up," he must be comfortable moving freely under you and laterally supple (meaning able and willing to bend his body and "give his face" to both sides). You started lateral work in the last chapter, and you've already taught your horse to flex at the poll and soften his jaw. Now, you'll begin to ask him to drive farther underneath himself with his hind legs, what dressage riders call "engaging the hindquarters."

Think again of that accordion, or of "shortening the wheelbase." You drive your horse's back end forward, while keeping his front end from extending farther forward. That means the only place for the "slack" to be taken out is in the middle—your horse's back lifts and rounds, which also lightens his shoulders, making them more maneuverable.

When done correctly, collection induces your horse to lower his head and neck for balance, the shoulders serving as a fulcrum as the hind end also comes under. If, instead, all you do is force your horse's head down by seesawing the reins, you get an artificial head set, with the hind end still strung out. If your horse were to trip at this point, he'd take a header! We saw the "peanut pushers" in Western pleasure for many years; the way

these horses moved represented an artificial lowering of the head.

The exercises in this chapter will enable you to begin work on collection (as you also polish your horse's steering—more on that in a moment). In general, transitions between speeds and between gaits are especially good for developing collection, particularly when the transition is from faster to slower.

Over time, you'll be striving for more and more "framing up," and asking your horse to hold that body position for longer periods. As with all new work, you must proceed incrementally and, in the beginning, be satisfied with one stride at a time. Collection requires new muscle development from your horse, just as *you* need to develop new muscles anytime you take up a new sport. If you push your horse too hard in the beginning, before his muscles are ready to maintain collection for longer periods, he'll get sore, which will make him resentful. Remember my "ride smart" advice from chapter 2—don't make what you want a chore for your horse! Make it relatively pleasant and doable, and his mental and physical comfort will translate into better progress overall.

I'll keep revisiting collection throughout the book as you continue to hone your skills. Developing collection is like peeling an onion—you work on one layer at a time, starting at the outer, rougher part, and working your way into finer and finer detail. (And, as you go along, you're bound to shed some tears!)

## Steering or Guiding

The goal of steering is to get your horse's feet to follow his nose. In other words, his nose—and not his shoulder—should lead all changes of direction. Your hands show your horse where you want him to go by tipping his nose that way; your legs enforce the directive by inducing his feet to follow accordingly.

By now, even if your horse is a youngster, he should be beyond the "90-day-colt" stage, assuming you've

A

B

C

**6.1 A–C** Degrees of collection

My horse is moving freely in A, but he's not collected or "framed up." Note his flat topline, his face in front of the vertical, and his overall "strung-out" look. In B I use my legs in neutral position to drive my horse forward into the "wall" of my hands, and what a difference! Note the rounded topline, the vertical face, and the overall look of collection. Responding to the same cues, in C my horse has further "shortened his wheelbase," carrying even more of his weight on his hind end and lightening his front end. Collection requires new muscle development in your horse, so don't ask for too much at one time. Work in increments.

**6.2 A & B** Hand position

A wide hand position for steering is appropriate when your horse is learning to be guided (A), but as he progresses, begin to carry your hands closer together (B), in preparation for the time when you'll transition him into a bridle (see p. 126) and ride him with one hand.

diligently done the Essentials work of chapter 5. This means the days of using your hands really wide in order to guide him are over (figs. 6.2 A & B). If you use your hands wide now, you'll be sabotaging your effort to get him to move with greater balance. Instead, your pull on the direct rein should be toward your hip—or, more specifically, toward the belt loop on the same side of your pants as the hand doing the pulling. At the same time, maintain enough pressure on your indirect rein to balance your horse. All this promotes a nose-first, on-the-hindquarters turn that's more balanced and collected (figs. 6.3 A–C).

At this stage in the game, the reins should be loose or drape except when steering or "checking" the horse's speed or headset. Work with sequences of tension and release, creating some pressure to correct your horse's frame when necessary, and then "giving" to reward his response. However, be sure not to throw your hands forward when giving the reins or to "giddy up." You're not carrying a mail pouch! If you throw your hands forward, you cause your horse to fall on his front end.

To use your hands properly, think about keeping them within an imaginary, 1-foot-square box centered over the saddle horn. As you and your horse progress over time, that box will begin to shrink. Eventually, when your horse is responding to the subtlest of cues, the box will be just a few inches square.

When using your legs to guide your horse, think in terms of gradients, as we discussed in the Leg Cues sidebar on p. 39. Start with light pressure, then move to firmer pressure, bumping, and even kicking or rolling your spur as needed. Horses can feel a fly on their side,

**6.3 A–C** Correct vs. incorrect direct rein

*Correct:* To turn your horse, pull the direct rein toward your side belt loop as I am demonstrating in A. At the same time, maintain enough pressure on the indirect rein to help balance your horse. Note I've maintained a straight line from the bit to my elbow. *Incorrect:* When turning, don't pull down or low as in B. It promotes heaviness on the forehand. In C, my direct rein pull is too low, plus my other hand is bringing the indirect rein across my horse's neck—both incorrect.

## It Ain't So

MYTH: **It's better to use "body English" like leaning to guide your horse than to use your reins.**

I run into this a lot in my clinics—for some reason, people think the less they use their reins, the better, so they try to throw their weight around to steer their horse. How you sit in the saddle is important, of course, but that doesn't mean you're doing your horse any favors by purposely changing your position on top of him. It just causes him to lean and become unbalanced in return, which isn't what you want and is uncomfortable for him.

Remember: your reins are there for a purpose, and it's okay to use them!

but they can become incredibly dull to leg pressure, especially if you consistently use more than you need. Always give your horse the chance to respond to the lightest pressure—yet move up to what you ultimately need to ensure a response.

At all times, strive to keep your horse between your hands and your legs. As I mentioned earlier, ultimately, you want *him* to be within an imaginary box created by your hands and legs. If he pushes his nose out, he bumps into the front wall of the box—your hands. If he bows out or falls in, he bumps into one side of the box or the other—your legs. If he gets strung out, his hind end hits the back of the box—both of your legs driving him forward.

Now I'll show you the exercises you can use to simultaneously work on collection and steering.

## Exercises: Baseball Diamond and Daisy

I'll describe these two exercises, then provide trouble-shooting information (because you'll be working to develop collection *and* steering in both).

As you work on these exercises, remember to "ask" for what you want with enough authority to command your horse's attention to get results, but not so vigorously that you cause him to worry. Scaring him only makes things worse: he'll become defensive, raise his head, and stiffen his jaw. This stiffness will travel throughout his body, resulting in the exact opposite of what you want, which is being light with supple responsiveness.

### Baseball Diamond

Set markers at each corner of an imaginary baseball diamond, at least 90 feet square (fig. 6.4). Your goal is to trot around the diamond while keeping your horse straight between your reins and legs, bending through the corners, and moving forward with energy and control.

Keep your horse on a relatively loose rein as much as possible. Start at home base, then trot in a straight

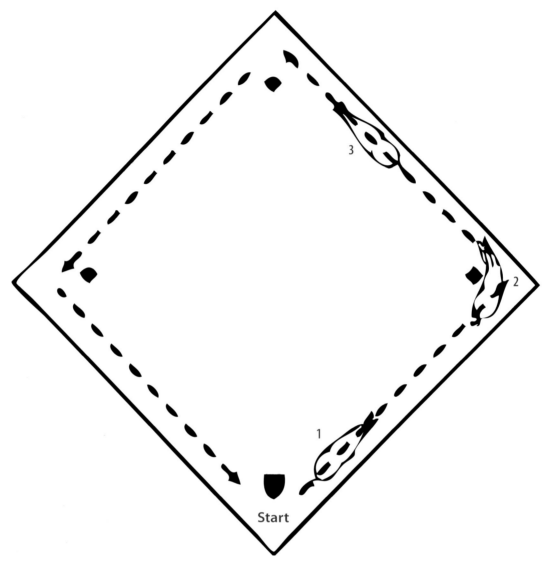

**6.4** The Baseball Diamond

Set markers at each corner of an imaginary diamond that's at least 90 feet square. Trot the diamond, keeping your horse straight between your reins and legs, bending through the corners, and moving forward with energy and control. Move on line toward first base, using both legs in neutral position or just behind it to drive your horse forward. As you approach first base, use light backward pressure on both reins to slow him a bit while driving with your seat to encourage collection. Use your inside (direct) rein and inside leg at neutral position to guide him through a tidy turn, supporting with your outside (indirect) rein and leg as necessary. Then align him and go to the lope only when you can do the exercise steering easily, with your horse balanced, keeping a steady pace, and staying straight on the straightaways. Work in both directions.

straight toward second base while encouraging him forward. Continue in this manner around the diamond. Be sure to work in both directions.

When you can go around with your horse balanced and steering easily, keeping a steady speed (not speeding up when the reins are loose) and staying straight on the straightaways, try it at a lope, again being sure to work in both directions.

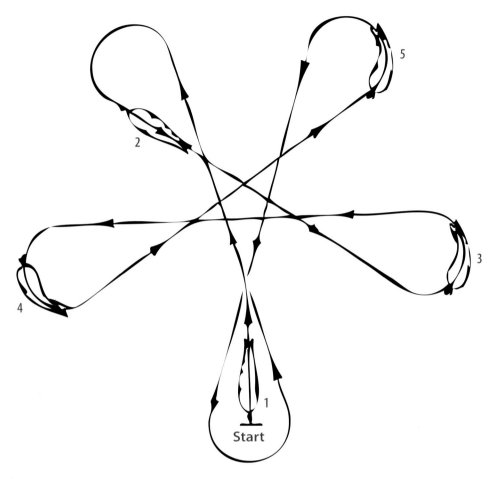

**6.5** The Daisy

This exercise has you ride a shape that approximates the "petals" of a "daisy." Begin at a trot; move through the center of the "daisy," and as you approach the far end of the "petal," pick up your reins and drive with your seat to ask your horse to collect. Then, tip his nose to the inside of the "petal." At the same time, apply your inside leg at the cinch (or slightly behind it), and use your outside leg just behind the cinch to keep his hind end from drifting as you bend him around a 180-degree turn. You should now be heading back through the center of the "daisy." Repeat the sequence each time you get to the far side of a "petal," always turning in the same direction and always using enough outside (indirect) rein to straighten your horse's body for the return trip through the center. When you've worked in both directions at the trot, try it at the lope, working one lead for awhile, then the other.

## Daisy

This exercise calls for you to ride a pattern that will approximate the petals of a daisy (fig. 6.5). Begin at a trot on a straight line. As you approach the far end of the "petal" (away from the center of the daisy), pick up your reins and simultaneously drive with your seat to draw your horse back onto his hind end, asking him to shorten his frame and collect.

Then tip his nose to the turn side and use the leg on the same side, at the cinch or just behind it, to bend him around 180 degrees so that you're heading back toward the *center* of the "daisy." Make sure you straighten your horse with your outside (indirect) rein and leg as you come out of the 180-degree turn, so you can drop him on a straight line through the center.

Repeat the sequence each time you get to the far

**6.6** "Checking up"
**Tying the reins loosely to the cinch can help your horse learn to stay off the bit— not leaning or pulling on your hands. Don't leave him standing, though; keep him moving around the pen, or on a longe line.**

You began work on softness in chapter 5 (Essential 1: Giving the Face), and you continued it in the collection work in this chapter. If, in spite of all that, your horse still doesn't seem to be "getting" that he must get off the bit and stay off it (instead he leans on your hands or pulls), it may be time to let him pull on himself for a while instead of you. "Checking him up" is a groundwork exercise done in a round pen that nicely accomplishes this goal. By working the horse with the reins secured to the saddle (a point with little to no "give") rather than in your hands (which are connected to your naturally elastic and moveable arms), you teach him that leaning on the bit or pulling on the reins is an exercise in futility.

Your horse should wear a plain, smooth-mouthed snaffle and his regular saddle. Take him to a small round pen (a 40- to 45-foot-diameter one is ideal, but whatever is handy and safe will do; you can even longe him checked up if you don't have

the appropriate enclosure). Tie the reins to the cinch rings or behind the cantle (fig. 6.6). Always begin with the reins quite loose so your horse's face is comfortably in front of the vertical. If he feels overly confined by the reins before he understands how this exercise works, he may become frightened and claustrophobic, even to the point of flipping himself over backward.

Once he begins to understand, however, gradually shorten the reins until his face is more or less at the vertical—perpendicular to the ground—as he moves around the pen. As he softens to the bit pressure, he may occasionally come behind the vertical as he walks. But do *not* tighten the reins so much that his face is behind the vertical at rest, or comes significantly behind the vertical, curling toward his chest, as he walks.

With the reins loosely tied at first, use your voice and body language to drive your horse forward at a

**6.7** "Checking up" (one side shorter)

**Shortening one rein an inch or two more than the other helps to improve lateral flexion. Readjust when changing direction. "Check your horse up" for short periods only, and follow with a riding session to see how he is doing.**

walk. Work in both directions, and when he seems relaxed and understands what you want, ask for a trot. Because it's a symmetrical gait, the trot is good for inducing relaxation. Spend time at this gait, frequently changing direction to avoid stressing your horse's legs. As he relaxes further and accepts the exercise, gradually shorten the reins (again, never tightening them so that his face is behind the vertical at rest).

Now work at both a trot and lope, again changing direction frequently. If your horse needs work on lateral flexion—"giving his face" to the side—shorten the inside rein an inch or two more than the outside, readjusting the reins each time you change direction (fig. 6.7).

Spend no more than a total of 10 minutes the first time you "check your horse up" in the round pen; remember that too much work before he's developed the musculature to support it will

make him sore and unhappy. Over time, gradually lengthen your round-pen sessions up to a maximum of about 20 minutes.

Always follow the round-pen checking up with a short ride to see what you've accomplished and to solidify the lesson in your horse's mind.

Note: some trainers advocate leaving a horse standing while checked up; *I don't*. I believe that in order to learn the lesson correctly, the horse should be softened in the face while engaging the hind end in motion. And, simply for safety's sake, he needs to be supervised.

In the future, you'll find that round-pen work at a steady trot is a great way to get the "fresh" off and relax your horse when he hasn't been ridden for a few days, or before showing. Work at the lope is good for getting a horse "evened up" so that his stiff (less bendable) side isn't as stiff, and his hollow (overly bendable) side isn't as hollow.

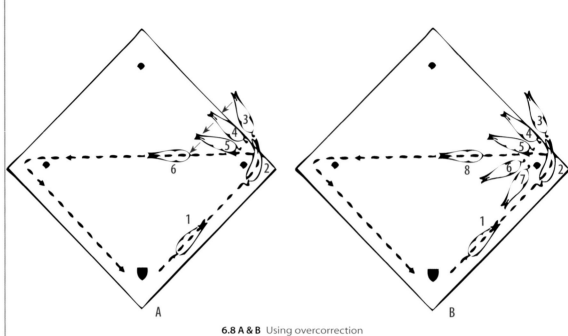

**6.8 A & B** Using overcorrection

In order to make an impression on a horse that persistently misbehaves or misunderstands your cues, you may need to *overcorrect* him. In Fig. 6.8 A we see the example of a horse (3) that continually drifts out on the Baseball Diamond as he rounds "first base" (perhaps because he is drawn by a magnet). Overcorrect his inappropriate action by immediately tipping his nose to the left with your direct rein, applying your indirect rein and outside leg at or just behind the cinch, and turning him 45 degrees *away* from the magnet while keeping his body fairly straight beneath you (4 & 5). Cut straight across the diamond, going from first base to third, skipping second entirely (6).

If your initial overcorrection of the horse's undesired action does not succeed, further up the ante (fig. 6.8 B). Using my first example: when the horse continues to drift out on the Baseball Diamond as he rounds first base, stop (3), and instead of turning him 45 degrees as in your previous overcorrection, this time use your indirect rein and outside leg more aggressively to turn a full 360 degrees before again cutting straight across to third base (4–8). The extra work will teach the horse to take the "easy" route—straight and on track—the next time around the Baseball Diamond.

Using varying degrees of overcorrection gets results because the horse learns that he has to work harder if he veers off track. It also helps get him "between the reins." Repeat the overcorrective measure until the horse properly performs the desired maneuver.

side of a "petal," always turning in the same direction and always using enough outside rein to straighten your horse's body for the return trip through the center of the "daisy."

Each time you go on the straight line through the middle, loosen the reins; each time you come to the far side and prepare to make the 180, use your reins and seat to ask your horse to engage his hocks and hind end; then tip his nose and make the small half-circle turn.

Your end tracks should approximate the petals of a daisy. When you've worked in both directions at the trot, try it at the lope, working one lead for a while, then the other.

Once your horse is confirmed in this exercise at the lope, you have a tool to return to if he gets a bit "on the muscle" when you start speeding up during your run-downs, or if he fails to go straight when you ask him to, or anticipates lead changes; we'll talk more about all this in upcoming chapters.

### ☞ Troubleshoot It

When the horse:

Over- or underbridles: When your horse curls his neck and tucks his chin to his chest (overbridling), use more leg and *less* hand. And, when he resists flexing at the poll and softening to the reins (underbridling), use more leg and *more* hand. If he still refuses to soften, stop him, and work his jaw by sliding the bit softly back and forth in his mouth until he does soften, back him up a few steps, then let him stand for a moment to think about it. (Note: if your horse really resists remaining soft in the face, try the exercise described in Checking Up, p. 74, to help him understand the concept of staying off the bit.)

Resists hind-end engagement: If he won't rock back on his hind end as you're preparing for a turn, push down on the balls of your feet and curl your seat under a bit. At the same time, raise your hands toward your lower rib cage and squeeze your shoulder blades together

as you pull back slightly on the reins, and bump with your legs. Even with your arms raised, though, be sure to maintain that straight line from the bit through your hands to your elbow; in other words, your hands should not come up on their own, which would break the line from bit to elbow.

Rushes: If your horse gets assertive and wants to go faster, ask for more collection by pushing with your seat and bumping with your legs in neutral position while "holding" with your reins. Then bring him back to the desired speed, guide him through a change of direction, and release the "extra" cues, allowing him to relax. Do this every time he speeds up. Extra collection and turning is hard work, so your horse will begin to associate rushing with working harder, and so be more willing to stay at the speed you choose.

Another approach is just to treat this "motoring on" as no big deal and go back to a circle, letting your horse go fast with his nose tipped to the inside, not arguing with him, until he relaxes and slows down on his own. Most horses eventually decide going fast just means more work. As you learned in the "ride smart" section of chapter 2 (p. 8), it's a bit of reverse psychology.

Breaks gait on the slowdown, or falls out of the lead at the lope: These are a result of your horse becoming unbalanced. Correct breaking gait by collecting him up more on the straight line—really drive his hind end up and get him balanced *before* going around the corner. For falling out of a lead, do the same but with an emphasis on using your outside leg a few inches behind neutral position to drive his rear end to the inside just a bit.

Leans: First, you need to be able to tell when your horse is leaning, and sometimes that's hard to feel. One good way is to check for a feeling of equal pressure from the saddle to your bottom. If you feel more weight or pressure in your left buttock than in your right, for example, your horse is leaning to the right and you're compensating. Sometimes riders don't compensate, and might therefore feel more pressure on their right buttock when their horse is leaning right. The "bottom line," so to speak, is that your weight should be equally distributed across your bottom!

Another way to tell when your horse is leaning is to check whether your hands are an equal distance from your horse's neck. If the distance from his neck to your right hand is shorter than that from his neck to your left hand, he's leaning to the right. Our own bodies often "know" before our minds that we're out of balance from the horse's leaning, and our body parts try to straighten things out.

If you find your horse leaning in, use your reins and legs to move him back under you, then release. For example, if he's leaning to the right, carry both your hands to the left while applying your right leg vigorously at or just behind the cinch. You'll probably find that you must reposition your horse numerous times on the straight lines before he begins to "savvy" the concept of staying straight. Your corrections can go from mild to a bit more assertive as the situation requires. At the far end of assertiveness, you may need to *overcorrect* to make your point (see p. 76).

# 7 | LEAD DEPARTURES, CIRCLES, SPINS

A lead departure into the lope is the first thing a judge sees when you start your run, so its correctness helps to form his or her first impression of you. This departure takes you right into your circles and spins, which are the very heart of a reining pattern. It can be a thrill to watch a well-trained horse lope and gallop picture-perfect circles, as there's so much going on with so little *appearing* to be going on. Meanwhile, the spins, along with slides, are among the glamour moves of reining, where speed and precision create the dramatic action that aficionados love.

In this chapter, I explain how to pick up the correct lead, then help you develop and polish your circles and spins.

## Lead Departures

As I mentioned above, because the lead departure is the entry point into your pattern, it helps set the tone for your run and establishes expectations—good or bad—in the judge's mind. If you pick up the wrong lead or trot first, it will cost dearly in penalty points. And, if these two reasons aren't enough to get your departures down pat, know that a good one can help prepare your horse to change leads later in the pattern.

### "Scoring"

To prepare to pick up a lead, put your horse in the correct frame and ask him to walk a few steps in that frame before you ask for the lope. In the reining world, we call this "scoring." It's good discipline overall, and it teaches your horse to "wait" for you to ask for the lope. In the future, when in the show pen, this will help him stay quiet in the center of the arena, as he won't anticipate loping off if he knows that sometimes he just walks when he's in the "lead-departure frame."

This lead-departure frame will seem a bit contorted to the horse at first, so be patient and give him time to understand what you want.

When you want the horse to pick up the left lead, tip his nose *and* hind end slightly to the left. (This sets him up to stride off on the left lead.) As you tip his nose to the left, also "pick up" his left shoulder, using the "key in the ignition" move (see p. 49). At the same time, bump with your right leg just behind neutral position to push his rear to the left (fig. 7.1). Don't "over-tip" either end; it should be about 50-50.

Now, with your horse in this slightly bent frame, walk him straight forward for several strides. This is hard to do and will take some practice. Be patient, accepting one step at a time until you can get two, then three, and so on.

### The Departure

To ask for the left-lead lope, keep the horse's frame the same as you use your right leg (still just behind neutral) more assertively (i.e., rolling or pressing with your spur if need be) and "kiss." (I use a kissing noise for my lead departures because I think it helps "lift" the horse into the lope— you may have a different verbal cue.) As you push him into the bridle, keep his nose tipped left, and don't let him trot—instead, think "lift" him into the lope. Don't release your reins, either; move him right up into the bridle.

Do not let your horse slam his rear back into your right foot as he strikes off into the lope, or he'll likely pick up the wrong lead. Keep him moving off your leg, as this is essential to getting a change later on. Note: if he won't move off your leg, he won't change leads, ever.

Be sure to work both sides equally (simply reverse all cues for right lead scoring and departure). Do a lot of scoring until your horse is completely comfortable and good at it. Then, always do it for a few strides before you ask for the lope, so that you get a good departure. It's good discipline for your horse, and for you. He won't rush into the lope, and you'll be indirectly working on your changes every time you lope off!

### Circles

Reining patterns typically call for large, fast circles (executed at a gallop), and small, slow circles (at a controlled lope). Circles on both leads are joined at the center of the arena with a change of lead.

**7.1** "Scoring"

**This is walking your horse in the "lead-departure" frame. It prepares him to take the correct lead and teaches him to wait for the cue to lope. I'm getting ready to ask him to pick up the left lead, so I've tipped his head and hip to the left, while lifting my left rein to pick up his left shoulder.**

Ideally, your horse should run his circles "framed-up" or collected (driving from behind, round through his topline, shoulders equally up, soft in the bridle) but on a slack—or better yet, draped—rein (fig. 7.2). He should change speeds dramatically (there should be a very clear difference between the "slow" and "fast" circles), with no apparent cue from you except maybe a slight change in your position. He should "hunt the circle" (meaning he truly understands what a circle is and is looking to stay on it of his own volition), and his lead and speed changes should be in the middle of the arena.

**7.2** "Hunting the circle"
**Your goal is for your horse to lope his circles framed-up on a slack rein, staying true to the track he's on—we call this "hunting the circle."**

**7.3** Collecting for speed changes
**In the beginning, always push your horse into the bridle before you ask him to downshift from his large, fast circle to his small, slow one. This helps to keep him from falling out of his lead.**

It sounds relatively easy, yet I think people spend more time working on circles than any other maneuver. You've done much already to set the stage for super circles. In chapter 6, you worked on steering by riding Baseball Diamond and Daisy (see pp. 71 and 73). You also worked on collection (or "framing-up") to encourage your horse to be soft in the face while he drives from behind and keeps both shoulders "standing up" equally (see p. 17). Now, as you take circles a step further, it's important to keep riding your horse up into the bridle more and more. You want him rounding up through the topline more quickly, needing fewer aids, and holding the framed-up position voluntarily for a few strides even after you "pitch him some slack" (give him the reins).

You also helped set the stage in chapter 5, where you worked on establishing a perfect circle while evening out the asymmetry of your horse.

What's left now is to fine-tune the shape of your circle; to get your horse to "hunt the circle"; and speed control. You'll work on each of these in turn, as well as continue to polish your steering, shoulder control, and collection.

For best results, work on three different sizes of circles: small, large, and extra-large. Small is about 60 feet in diameter; large is about 120 feet; and when you have the space, extra-large is about 150 feet.

Keep in mind that the smaller the circle, the more difficult it is for your horse to hold himself framed-up, so don't push him on the small circles in the beginning. Give him some time to gain strength and understanding on the larger circles and work on the smaller circles only for short periods until he's more sure of himself.

When you're working on moving from a larger, faster circle to a smaller, slower one, it's best to have your horse a little tired so he'll be more open to the idea of slowing down (more of that "making the right thing easy," p. 6). Always slow down in the large circle for a few strides *before* directing your horse onto the smaller circle. If you start a smaller circle as you're slowing down or *directly after*, your horse will begin to anticipate it, and before long, he'll drop his shoulder and lean in every time you ask him to slow down.

In the beginning, always gather your horse up a bit by bumping with your legs in neutral position to push him into the bridle while you're on the large circle and *before* you ask him to slow down; this way, he won't fall out of his lead (fig. 7.3). With a hot horse, slow down at the center of the arena on every circle, then "break down" (gradually go through the gears from the lope, to the trot, to the walk, then halt) and sit there quietly for a while. This trains him to be on the lookout for a slowdown and a rest at the center of the pen, which makes this a good place to be in his mind. This, in turn, will pay big dividends when you're showing by helping to keep him from ignoring your slowdown cues or anticipating lead changes.

Obviously, ride your circles equally in both directions, so your horse develops the same on each lead.

In this chapter I work first on fine-tuning the shape of your circle ("rounding" it) using Baseball Diamond as a guide (see p. 71). Then I show you how to encourage your horse to "hunt the circle" on his own, using the exercise, Cutting the Pie. Lastly, I work on handling speed and changes in speed, followed by troubleshooting tips.

### "Rounding" the Circle

In the chapter 6 exercise Baseball Diamond, you worked on steering by leaving out a base and cutting across to overcorrect a drift. Now, to perfect the roundness of your circles, ride the full diamond on a curving line. In other words, ride a perfect circle, using the four corners of the diamond as a guide to keep your circle from shrinking or bulging to become oblong, pear-shaped, or otherwise misshapen (fig. 7.4).

For best results, place a visual marker, such as a traffic cone, at each corner of the diamond. As you round

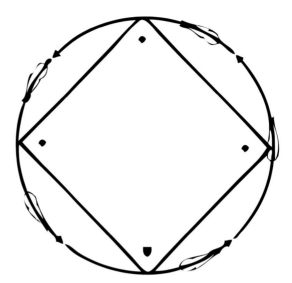

**7.4** Perfecting circle shape

**To perfect the roundness of your circles, use the Baseball Diamond again (see p. 71). Ride the diamond on a curving line at the lope, using the four "bases" as a guide to keep your circle from shrinking or bulging out. As you round each base, strive to make a perfectly curved track to the next base, then round that base the same way. This is how you "build" a perfect circle. Be sure to work equally on both leads. Over time, the feeling of riding a perfectly shaped circle will become second nature to you and your horse.**

the marker at a lope, strive to make a perfectly curved track to the next corner, then round that corner the same way you rounded the one before. In this way, you "build" a perfect circle.

Be sure to work equally on both leads. Over time, the feeling of riding a perfectly shaped circle will become second nature to you and your horse.

### Cutting the Pie

When your horse is "hunting the circle" you've put him on, he's on the same page as you. He's looking in the direction he's going and staying true to the circle, even on a loose rein. If, instead, he's looking over at the barn and thinking that's where he'd rather be, that's where he's going to go when you give him slack in the rein. He'll bow or drift out, ruining the symmetry of the circle.

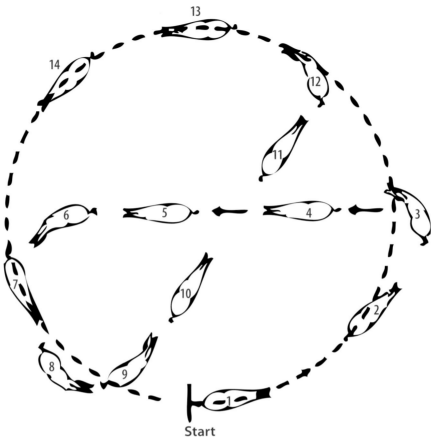

13

14

12

11

6 5 4 3

7

10

2

8 9

1

**Start**

**7.5** Cutting the Pie

Teach your horse to "hunt the circle" (voluntarily stay on track, without drifting in or out) by using this exercise. Put your horse on a lope circle, then give him a loose rein. If he drifts (2), let him go for a few strides, then with both hands moving toward your inside belt loop, steer him on a straight line through the center of the circle (3–5) to the far side of it, and pick up the track of the circle again (6 & 7). Then turn him loose again. If he drifts, repeat the correction (8–11). This way, *you're* not continuously holding him on the circle—you're training *him* to do it. Work equally on both leads.

When this happens, fix it by Cutting the Pie. Let him go ahead and drift...for a few strides, anyway. Then, with both hands moving toward your inside belt loop, steer him on a straight line through the center of the circle to the far side of it (as if cutting through the center of a pie), and pick up the track of the circle again, traveling in the same direction as you were. Put him on a loose rein again; if he drifts off course, guide him through the center of the circle again, picking up the track again on the far side. Viewed from above, your track should look roughly like a pie cut across in many places (fig. 7.5).

Any time your horse is actually "hunting the circle" with his ears and nose, just sit quietly; this becomes his reward. But when he starts to drift, cut through the center again. What you're doing is putting him back on the circle whenever he strays, but not continuously *holding* him on the circle. You're training *him* to do it.

Again, work equally on both leads. If you're diligent with this exercise, over time your horse *will* begin to "hunt the circle" consistently, so that only a minimum of reining from you is necessary.

## Controlling Speed

You've been working all along on encouraging your horse to stay framed-up even when you put slack in the reins. By now he should be rounding up well and holding the position on his own for a few strides after you pitch him slack.

Now, as you begin to ask for more speed, his "wheels will begin to wobble," so to speak. He'll get out of frame—his head and neck will come up, his back will hollow, and his hind legs will trail out behind. This is natural as speed increases. Have you ever seen a horse framed-up as he's running free? Or as he's running away? Neither have I. So we have to teach our horses how to handle speed both mentally and physically.

If your horse gets excited and wants to run off when you add a gear to your large circles, don't make a big fuss. Just let him go at the higher speed for a while, keeping his nose tipped to the inside so his inside shoulder stays up and he's not running off with you. As the thrill wears off and he realizes no one is fighting him to slow down, he'll reconsider. When he begins to feel as if he *wants* to slow down (softening in the face and beginning to ease off on the speed), *reinforce* that idea for him. Take a deep breath, then let it out slowly (humming or otherwise making your breath audible—which helps you relax in a way your horse can feel) and "melt" in the saddle. He'll continue to think it's *his* idea as he slows down. When this happens, lope a slow circle (not necessarily a smaller one—remember, you don't want him to equate slowing down with cutting in to a smaller circle). Then break him down softly to a trot, then walk, then "Whoa," then back up a few steps. Let him rest for a moment.

Once he realizes that volunteering to lope fast winds up being a lot of work, he'll be only too happy to slow down when you ask. At this point, he'll be handling speed well mentally, so advance to work on "framing him up" (drive his rear end up under him with your legs while softening his jaw with the reins) more and more while going fast. Do this just a few strides at a time, though, until he no longer resists it, and can hold the rounded position for longer periods of time on his own.

### ☞ Troubleshoot It

When the horse:

Refuses to slow down: Don't jerk on the reins. Instead, sit down in the saddle, with your shoulders square, and pull assertively on the reins to draw him down "through the gears" to a stop. Don't use more rein pressure than is needed, but use enough to get the job done promptly. Release pressure for a moment when he does stop, to reward his response. Then back him a few steps, stop, and stand for a moment so he can think about it.

Falls out of lead when slowing: Do these things before you ask him to slow: keeping his nose tipped to the inside, gather him up by driving him onto the bit with your legs and push his hind end a bit to the inside by bumping just behind neutral position with your outside leg. This positions his body to remain on the correct lead and makes it hard for him to break gait or switch leads.

Drifts off track (your "power steering" fails): Overcorrect by cutting across to the other side of the circle, as you learned in Cutting the Pie.

Leans to the inside, falls into the circle, drops his inside shoulder: This is most likely to happen on the left lead (his "stiff" direction, as you'll recall from chapter 2, p. 18) when he's at the point in the circle that's farthest from his favorite magnet. By moving toward the magnet, he cuts in and makes the circle smaller. To fix it, don't make any small, slow circles for awhile. Ride only large, fast and large, slow circles. Then, the moment you feel him starting to drop his shoulder and pull in, try the exercise Backing-in-a-Circle (see p. 86).

In this exercise, which corrects your horse when he drops his inside shoulder, leans in, or cuts in on a circle, you bring him to a stop, then back him right up in a small circle just inside the track he was just on. Back the horse at least one revolution—more if necessary—until he is "trying," and not "arguing."

This is one of my favorite exercises for two reasons. First, it's fabulous for gaining control of your horse's shoulders. Backing-up on a circle is hard, hard work, so it really makes him think twice about dropping that shoulder in the first place.

Second, it makes him more supple and "quiet-minded" in general, so it supports your overall training goals.

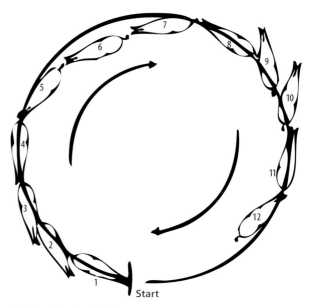

**7.6** Backing-in-a-Circle

*Here's How*

Take a look at fig. 7.6. The moment you feel your horse drop his shoulder and cut in on the circle, gently break him down to a stop (1). As you do, carry both reins toward the outside of the circle, being sure to lift his inside shoulder with the "key in the ignition" twist of the wrist of your inside hand.

Once he's stopped, put him in reverse and back him up on the same circle you were just on, only much smaller (2–6). As you back up:

Tip his nose to the inside of the circle using the "key in the ignition" twist of your inside hand, which will help keep his inside shoulder from dropping.

Pull both his shoulders to the outside and "stand them up straight" by carrying both your hands slightly to the outside.

Keep his hind end to the inside by bumping with your outside leg just behind neutral position.

All this requires serious concentration and coordination on your part and that of your horse. If you find it too difficult in the beginning and his hindquarters drift back out or he balks (7), instead just back up for two steps (8), move his shoulders out for two steps (9 & 10), then back up straight for two steps (11). Then move his rear end in for two steps (12), then back straight for two steps. Gradually, over time, try to make the moves simultaneous—which becomes a circle.

Now look at how I'm handling the exercise in the photos (figs. 7.7 A–D). Once you've perfected this exercise, it will give you control of the horse's shoulders that no other exercise can.

Be sure to work in both directions, as need be.

After you've caught your horse cutting in and consequently backed him around until he "stands his shoulders up" a few times, you'll actually feel him begin to consciously make the choice *not* to fall in when he gets on that far side of the circle away from the barn. You're teaching him how to make the right (but difficult) choice by making the alternative (backing in a circle) even more difficult. (You can also use this to correct your horse when he drops his shoulder and "dives" into the new direction after a lead change, as you'll learn in chapter 9.)

A

B

C

D

**7.7 A–D** Backing in a Circle

Going to the left, I tip my horse's nose to the inside using the "key in the ignition" twist of my left hand; this keeps his inside shoulder from dropping. I also carry both hands somewhat to the outside, to pull both his shoulders slightly to the outside of the circle. As we continue backing-up, I bump with my outside leg just behind neutral position to move his hind end to the inside of the circle while continuing to pull his shoulders to the outside. This type of backup is hard work for your horse, so it is a good way to "make the right thing easy and the wrong thing difficult." For example, initiate it when he drops his inside shoulder or cuts in on a circle, and he'll soon learn that "standing up" and staying true to the track is the better choice! This exercise helps you develop excellent control of your horse's shoulders—something that will benefit you in all maneuvers.

## Spins

A dynamic, judge-pleasing spin is performed on a loose rein, with the horse's nose tipped slightly in the direction of the turn. The horse is "hunting" the spin—meaning he's doing it willingly—and his neck is low. His outside front foot crosses over his inside front, and he steps rapidly, smoothly, and with cadence. He pivots on his inside hind foot (although both hind feet can move within a small area without penalty). At the end, he stops right on the mark, without losing balance or requiring excessive help from his rider.

The best way to think of a spin is *forward motion redirected around.* You *step your horse forward* into a spin, which helps him differentiate cues from those that ask for a backup or a roll-back. Stepping forward into the spin also reinforces that you want him to "drive" into the spin, with his shoulders upright and even. Ultimately, you should be able to ask your horse to speed up his spin with a "cluck," and he should remain in the spin without visible cueing from you until you say "Whoa."

To set the stage for spinning, you worked on getting your horse to step his front end around by drawing a circle tighter and then stepping across in Essential 7: Pivoting on the Hind End (p. 65). Now, you start building speed as you add more control, cadence, and precision.

First I'll share an easy way to get a correct spin started. Then, I'll give you an exercise for improving your spins, plus offer some troubleshooting tips.

The chapter ends with two more exercises: one that helps build cadence—Trot into the Spin—and an advanced exercise—Counter-Arc with the Spin—that will improve the straightness of your horse's body and the levelness of his neck.

Three important caveats before you get started. First, before your horse is in the bridle (see more on riding in a snaffle on p. 26, and putting your horse in the bridle on p. 126), think in terms of starting your spin with the inside (direct) rein, and speeding it up with your outside (indirect) rein and, if necessary, your out-

side leg, rather than dragging your horse around with your inside rein—an extremely common mistake.

Second, if your horse isn't spinning properly, it's usually because he's not moving off—you guessed it—your outside rein and leg! When this happens, don't just go "faster, wronger." Instead, stop and fix what isn't working (I'll talk more about this in the troubleshooting section on p. 92).

And third, *never* punish your horse during a spin. If something goes wrong, stop and fix what isn't working, then return to the spin, *letting* him turn and not forcing or intimidating him into it. This is essential if you want to make sure the spin never becomes something he dreads and tries to "hide" from. An ounce of prevention is worth a backhoe's ton of cure, here.

### An Easy Start

With these caveats in mind, let's get started. As you did when first teaching your horse to step his front end around in a pivot, work in a corner of your arena if possible (fig. 7.8). Note: in large, high-ceilinged barns you can often use an alleyway or aisle for the same purpose. If you're later practicing spinning out on the trail, use whatever visual barriers are available—tree lines, bushes, creeks—to stay oriented and provide visual boundaries.

Start your spin in the corner. Don't worry at all about speed at this point; correct form is what you're after now, and you can build speed later. So go only as fast as you can control and maintain correct form.

I'll break the cues down individually, but of course you apply them more or less simultaneously:

- Begin by closing both legs in neutral position to drive your horse forward toward one wall of the corner (because, remember, a spin is forward motion redirected around).
- Use your inside (direct) rein to tip your horse's nose slightly in the direction of the turn. (That rein must *not*, however, *pull* his head into the turn.)

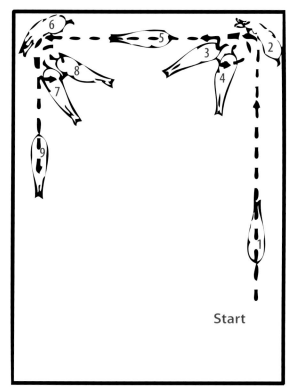

**7.8** Spin in the corner

**An easy way to start a spin is in a corner of your arena. Ride through a corner, and as you start to come out of it, position your horse so you can start the spin right back into the corner. This way, the first half of the spin is contained by the corner.**

▶ Close your outside (indirect) rein on your horse's neck, with a bit of backward pressure (that is, toward your belly button). Be sure not to cross this rein over his withers, however, or apply too much backward pressure to it, or your horse will counter-arc (bend away from the direction of the turn).

▶ With your *outside leg*, apply pressure at the cinch to help drive your horse's front end across and into the spin.

If your horse resists moving off your outside leg and rein, stop turning and reinforce his understanding of lateral movement by sidepassing him away from that same leg and rein. He should know how to do this from Essential 6: Moving Off Your Leg (p. 59). If

need be, review how to sidepass. As you do, be sure to "keep control of his face" (in other words, keep his jaw soft, his nose tipped, and his head properly positioned—not raised). After you get him "un-stuck," return to the spin.

When you start, think in 180-degree increments. After the first 180 degrees of the spin, you have the two sides of the arena corner to help contain and guide your horse through the second 180. Keep going like this just a few times, then reverse all cues to initiate a spin in the opposite direction.

Almost from the beginning of learning spins, practice counting every revolution of the spin, so it becomes habitual; this way, you'll never forget to do so at a show (when you must spin a set number of revolutions—no more and no less). So, no matter how marginal your early spins are, as you come around to your starting place the first time, say, "That's one." The next time around, say, "That's two." And so on.

### Improving the Spin

You've got a spin started; now let's work on perfecting it. This next exercise, a repeating combination of spinning and sidepassing along the arena fence, will get your horse driving and moving more freely in the spin (figs. 7.9 A–G).

▶ Start with your horse about 3 feet away from the fence, parallel to it, with his right shoulder closest to the fence.

▶ Begin a spin to the left, into the fence, and continue for one-and-a-quarter revolutions, so that when you stop you are perpendicular to the fence and facing into it.

▶ Now use your right (indirect) rein and leg to sidepass down the fence to the left, keeping your horse's body straight so he is perpendicular to the fence. Continue sidepassing until your horse is moving freely off your right rein and leg.

**7.9 A–G** Spin and sidepass

This sequence shows a spin started into the fence and combined with sidepassing as needed to correct resistance. Because a spin is forward motion redirected around, begin by closing both your legs in neutral position to drive your horse forward. Use your fence-side (direct) rein to tip (but *do not* pull!) your horse's nose in the direction of the turn, as you close your indirect rein on his neck with a bit of backward pressure (be sure not to cross the rein over his withers, however). With

G

your outside leg, apply pressure at the cinch to drive his front end around (A–C). My horse's body is arced in the direction of the spin as he comes around, and his jaw is soft and flexed. I keep him stepping around with correct form; note how soft the rein pressure is (D). Always go only as fast as you can maintain correct form. As my horse finishes the first revolution, I can continue spinning if he stays light and willing, gradually building up to two-and-a-quarter and then three-and-a-quarter revolutions. If he begins to resist moving off my outside leg and rein, I stop turning and reinforce his understanding of lateral movement, using the fence: keep his head positioned toward the fence with your reins, then use your outside (here,

right) leg in neutral position to ask him to step laterally to the left (E & F). After he's "remembered" how to move off your leg and rein, make a one-quarter turn and walk off in the opposite direction (G).

As soon as he's relaxed, tip his nose toward the fence with your direct rein and start all over again, spinning in the opposite direction from when you started. If he gets "sticky," simply sidepass him along the fence again (this time going in the opposite direction from the first sidepass), and you're set up to begin spinning again in the original direction. You're not "changing the subject" by alternating directions like this. You're just working both sides back and forth until they both improve.

- Then, turn your horse a quarter turn to the right so that he's parallel to the fence again, but facing in the opposite direction from before (now his left shoulder will be closest to the fence).
- Maintaining that 3-foot distance, walk along the fence keeping your horse's body parallel to the fence.
- Begin a spin to the left, into the fence, and continue for one-and-one-quarter revolutions, so that you stop while facing the fence, perpendicular to it.
- Use your right rein and leg to sidepass down the fence to the left.

When you can do all this fluidly, so that your horse is moving willingly off your rein and leg either way in the sidepass, increase the number of revolutions in the spin to two-and-a-quarter before sidepassing, then move up to three-and-a-quarter.

### ☛ Troubleshoot It

When the horse:

Runs in a circle instead of spinning: Stop your horse, then use the sidepass to remind him how to move laterally off your leg and rein. If you had been trying to spin to the right, sidepass him to the right until he's moving willingly off your left rein and leg, then resume the spin.

Doesn't keep his hind end in one spot: This means your horse's shoulders are "stuck." Get them "driving" by moving him in a counter-arc circle—Essential 3: Walking the Counter-Arc Circle (p. 52). (If need be, review this Essential.) Ride the counter-arc circle in both directions to get his shoulders moving freely, then return to your spin work.

Migrates (that is, the spin "corkscrews"): Your horse will usually corkscrew toward a magnet, such as the barn. To correct this, get the first half (180 degrees) of the spin started going toward the barn, then counter-arc the second 180 degrees so that he's moving his shoul-

ders away from the magnet. So if you're spinning to the right, counter-arc by tipping your horse's nose a bit left and driving his shoulders around clockwise (the same direction you were turning). His front end should make a larger circle than his rear end. Be sure not to let his shoulders fall to the right, but rather "stand them up" straight—upright and even—by thinking more "sidepass" for that second 180 degrees.

You are now back to your starting point; tip your horse's nose in the direction of the turn again, and go another 180 degrees. You'll probably feel his shoulders stop moving again, so tip his nose to the outside again and sidepass him for another 180 degrees. Continue like this in 180-degree increments until he steps all the way around.

If he still persists in corkscrewing, overcorrect by coming out of the spin for a moment to push him straight ahead, directly away from the magnet. Then resume the spin in the same direction as before.

Moves his hind end too much: Use your outside leg just behind neutral to push his hindquarters back into position. Also, because much of your hind end trouble comes from the shoulders not "driving" properly, do plenty of those counter-arc circles to reinforce shoulder control (see p. 52).

Leaves the spin by stepping forward: Draw him back with pressure on both reins. If he fights your hands, don't simply pull harder. Instead, keep the same degree of tension while you bump insistently with your outside leg at the cinch.

Steps backward or doesn't cross over in front: Push him forward with both legs in neutral position, ease off a bit on the reins, and use your outside leg a bit more aggressively at the cinch.

Gets "sticky" in the spin: Do *not* resort to overpulling on that inside (direct) rein! Instead, use your outside leg more vigorously at the cinch and "cluck" rhythmically for cadence. If need be, go back to spinning in the corner of your arena and build momentum in 180-degree increments. Or revisit the one-and-one-quarter turns into the fence followed by a sidepass that we discussed earlier—see Improving the Spin, p. 89.

Gets stiff or rigid in the spin: Drive your horse forward into a circle and use your legs in neutral position to push him into your hands to soften him in the face, then go back to the spin.

Gets his front legs too far out in front of him: Use pressure on both reins to draw him back slightly, while bumping with your outside leg at the cinch to continue to ask for the spin.

## Exercises: Trot into the Spin and Counter-Arc with the Spin

The first of these two exercises will help your horse build cadence; the second, more advanced one will improve his start into the spin, plus get him straighter and flatter (i.e., with a lower profile) as he spins.

### Trot into the Spin

This exercise uses the natural "one-two, one-two" timing of the trot to build greater cadence into your spins. Begin by trotting your horse in a small circle about 20 feet in diameter. As you circle, keep the trot cadence in your head by saying "step, step, step, step" in time with your horse's strides. Also, use both legs in neutral position to drive your horse into your hands, so that he's soft in the face, and use your inside (direct) rein to keep his nose tipped slightly to the inside of the circle.

Then, *without stopping first*, draw your horse into a spin. Strive to keep the exact same impulsion and cadence, and maintain the slight tip of your horse's head in the direction of the spin, plus his softness in the face.

## It Ain't So

MYTH: I need to worry about which hind foot my horse is planting in the spin.

I don't think I've given a clinic anywhere in the world where the question of which hind foot to plant hasn't come up. When I start working on the spin, I don't concern myself about which hind foot my horse is pivoting on. That's because it's not about the pivot foot, and it's all about the shoulders driving. When those shoulders are driving properly, my horse will be pivoting on his inside hind foot. Some horses shift back and forth between the two hind feet, and that's okay, too. If your horse pivots on his outside hind foot, it means he's too rocked back, not driving with his outside shoulder, and lying against your outside leg. (And, it's usually worse in a spin to the right because of the natural asymmetry of horses—see p. 18.)

Make sure he starts the spin as soon as you close your outside (indirect) rein on his neck and apply your outside leg at the cinch—don't let him trot another half circle before beginning to cross over with his front legs.

Let him spin a couple of revolutions, then drive him up even more into the bridle and take him onto the small trot circle, still maintaining that same "one-two" cadence. Don't let him lope; keep him at a trot. When you ride him onto the small circle, make sure his outside shoulder is up underneath him and "driving." If it is, there won't be excessive bend anywhere in his body, and the bend he does have will be true to the arc of the small circle you're on.

Be sure to work equally in both directions.

### Counter-Arc with the Spin

This is a much more advanced exercise, so be sure your horse is relatively fluent in spinning and sidepassing before you attempt it. You go from a spin directly into a counter-arc circle in the same direction, then initiate a spin in the opposite direction right out of the counter-arc circle (fig. 7.10).

This exercise fine-tunes your horse's position going into the spin, plus helps him learn to stay straight and flat (i.e., hold his head low) during the spin.

Start by walking your horse in a perfect circle to the right, about 15 feet in diameter, keeping his nose tipped slightly to the inside. Ask him to begin a spin by drawing the inside (direct) rein toward your right-side belt loop and close your outside (indirect) rein toward your horse's neck with a bit of backward pressure, while bumping with your left leg at the cinch.

As he spins, the moment you feel him lagging or resisting in any way (which tells you he isn't moving as fluidly as he should off your outside leg and rein), use pressure on your outside (indirect) rein to change the tip of his nose from the inside to the outside, and begin bumping aggressively with your outside leg in neutral position to drive him around in a large (about 30 to 40 feet in diameter) counter-arc circle—just as I described in the second troubleshooting tip on p. 92. It should feel as if he's sidepassing on a circle, with his shoulders up, even, and driving; his front legs crossing over; and his face soft in the bridle.

When your horse is moving around like this nicely, reverse your cues to ask him to hesitate for an instant, then go directly into a spin in the opposite direction. His body, bent to the outside as it was on the counter-arc circle, will be perfectly positioned to begin the new spin.

Continue to spin in the new direction until he begins to lag, then go right into a counter-arc circle in the same direction. When he's moving well in the counter-arc circle, return to spinning in the original direction. And so on.

### 7.10 Spin and counter-arc

I use this counter-arc exercise to correct resistance in the spin. Ask your horse to begin the spin (1–4), and the moment you feel that he isn't moving fluidly off your outside leg and rein (5–7), use pressure on your outside (indirect) rein to change the tip of his nose from the inside to the outside (8 & 9), and begin bumping aggressively with your outside (in this case, left) leg in neutral position to drive him around in a large counter-arc circle (10–14). He should feel as if he is sidepassing on the circle. When he's doing so nicely, reverse your cues to ask him to hesitate for an instant, then go directly into a spin in the opposite direction (15). His body, bent as it was on the counter-arc circle, will be perfectly positioned to begin the new spin. Work back and forth with this exercise to get both your right and left spins evened up, flat, and fluid.

# 8
# STOP, BACK, ROLLBACK

Quick—what's the image that comes to mind when you think "reining"? It's the sliding stop, isn't it? The stop is what each pattern builds toward, and it's what makes spectators hold their breath—then burst into applause. Stops can't be faked, but they can certainly be improved upon. I'll focus on exactly that throughout most of this chapter.

At a show, your rundown and your stop will be judged in conjunction with a backup or a rollback. In other words, depending on where you are in a pattern, you'll receive one score for a rundown, a stop, and a backup; or a rundown, a stop, and a rollback.

So I'll cover the backup and the rollback in this chapter, as well as the stop, and then I'll give you a great strategy for combining all three maneuvers.

## Stopping, Sliding

The stop is not only reining's most dramatic maneuver, it's also the most important in terms of scoring points. That's because patterns typically include three or four stops, as compared to two each for spins and

lead changes. When you can develop a solid, reliable stop with your horse, you're on your way to doing well in the show pen.

In the ideal sliding stop, the horse is galloping at top speed and framed-up with his back round. Then, with no visible cue from the rider, his hind end drops. Meanwhile, his front end maintains the cadence of his striding so that he continues to "run with it," straight and true, pulling himself along with his front legs, right to the end of the stop (figs. 8.1 A & B).

From the saddle, a sliding stop feels amazingly smooth, and not abrupt the way you might expect. The horse's back end just falls out from under you, causing your seat to tuck a bit and your spine to curve as the two of you melt into and glide along the ground. It's an amazing feeling, and one I'm going to help you achieve.

In this section, I'll revisit what you already learned about "Whoa," plus I'll give you a couple of other strategies to try if your horse is still resisting stopping.

Then I'll teach you three exercises (Whoa-Back, "Fencing," and Runarounds) to improve your horse's stop and begin to encourage him to slide.

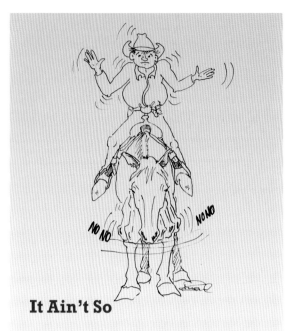

## It Ain't So

**MYTH:** I need to worry about where my horse's feet are when I say "Whoa."

I tell my students *not* to worry about this. I do so because if you do, you'll be so focused on *his feet* that you won't be riding your horse to the stop, and the latter is far more important. Ultimately, knowing where your horse's feet are at any given moment is a feeling you get (after a lot of time in the saddle!) in the seat of your pants.

In the meantime, if you just take a deep breath, let it out steadily, and say "Whoa" at the bottom of that breath, you'll almost always be asking for the stop when your horse's body is in the best position to slide. As a bonus, you'll stay nice and relaxed and you won't brace, which will help your horse to stay soft, too.

**8.1 A & B** A good vs. "wimpy" stop
*Good:* In A, my horse is round through his topline and really using his hind end. *Wimpy:* In B, my horse isn't "getting into the ground" the way we want him to because I didn't ride him all the way to the stop.

Note: Now's a good time to start using skid boots to protect your horse's hind fetlocks from getting friction burns, and have your farrier put sliding plates on his hind feet. The plates won't *cause* him to slide, but they'll sure make it *easier* for him to do so—and, as you'll recall from chapter 2, making what we ask easy for the horse is a "smart rider" basic.

### Revisiting "Whoa"

From your foundation work on the Essentials in chapter

**8.2** Correct body position in the stop
**I'm sitting deep and thinking "abdominal crunch" rather than leaning back. My heels are down, and my hands are soft and slow as they "ask" fluidly for the stop.**

5, your horse should by now stop going forward when he hears the word "Whoa." There's a lot of horsemanship going on in a stop, however, so let's review some of the most common mistakes riders make to double-check that *you're* not making any of them (fig. 8.2). They are:

Not actively riding until you say "Whoa." You must keep riding your horse forward right up to the moment that you ask him to stop; otherwise, he won't be driving with his rear end up into the stop, which is what causes his shoulders to lift so he can slide. Instead, he'll either "scotch" ("stutter-stop" because he's anticipating the stop) or drop his shoulders and pitch you forward.

Prematurely stopping the horse's motion. Sit and ride all the way to the bottom of the stop, and don't brace with your body or you'll compromise the quality of his stop. At the end of the stop, release everything and relax—your horse needs that release to recognize and be rewarded for achieving what you've asked of him.

Not saying "Whoa" with authority and conviction. If you're tentative, your horse will be tentative, too.

Pulling the reins *before* or *as you say* "Whoa." This prevents your horse from learning to stop at "Whoa." Instead, say "Whoa," then count "one, and..." before putting tension on the reins, if necessary.

Being too quick with your hands. If you want your horse to respond fluidly, you must "ask" fluidly.

Balancing yourself on the reins. This destroys communication and numbs your horse's response to you. (Go back to chapter 4, and review the importance of an independent seat, p. 35.)

Looking down at the spot where you want to stop. Look up as you run toward a stop; this gives your horse the feeling he's going to be running forever, which in turn helps him to run "uphill" (as opposed to heavy on his forehand). If, instead, you're looking down at the ground where you plan to stop, you ride "downhill" to that spot, which causes him to drop his front end as he puts on the brakes.

Leaning back, instead of just sitting deep and thinking *abdominal crunch* when you say "Whoa." Leaning throws your horse off balance.

Letting your toes point down or letting your feet get behind you. This can result in getting what we call "dashboarded"—that is, thrown forward, out of position.

Losing your balance or bracing yourself in anticipation of an imperfect stop. This causes your horse to lose *his* balance or brace *himself*, which automatically degrades his stop. In other words, physically anticipating a bad stop becomes a self-fulfilling prophecy.

Not correcting a lean—your own or your horse's. When you lean, it causes your horse to lean, and when he does, he'll stop crookedly.

Letting your horse pull on the reins as he runs (which causes him to be heavy in the front end) or accelerate on his own (a blatant disobedience that will escalate if left unchecked). You want him soft in the bridle and responding to your cues at all times.

### Extra Stopping Help

If you're doing everything right and your horse still needs more reinforcement to stop, try this. Meet his forward motion by taking the slack out of the reins and holding softly but firmly and pull steadily until he does stop. Then continue the pressure to rock him back (back up) several steps, release all pressure, let him rest, and give him a pat. We call this "drawing a horse into the ground."

How you maintain the rein pressure is critical: don't lock your hands down on either side of the saddle horn; this just causes him to brace on his front end. Instead, your hands should be at your belt level as they pull softly, yet insistently until he stops.

If he *still* doesn't want to stop, you can't force him to, but you can turn him abruptly into a (safe) fence if he ignores the cue to "Whoa." Obviously, the ultimate goal is for your horse to stop and rock back when you say "Whoa." But in the beginning, a turn into the fence can make him begin to "hunt the stop" (desire to stop of his own volition) much more than simply pulling on both reins. That's because a sudden deceleration or turn is a lot more work than a plain stop. It's also a bit disarming, and he can't brace against it the way he can against a pull straight back on both reins.

To accomplish this "correcting" turn into the fence, sit deep in the saddle (with pressure on the balls of your feet and your heels down) and pull the fence-side rein toward your side belt loop, balancing that pressure by holding the other rein softly until your horse slows, stops, shifts his weight back on his hind end, and turns into the fence. You want your horse to have his weight on his hind end as he turns, and not lurch into the fence shoulder-first.

Now let's move on to some "stop-refining" exercises.

### The Whoa-Back

In this exercise, you stop your horse, ask him to further soften to your hands, then back him up several times in succession in response to "Whoa." In this way, the idea that "Whoa" means *no forward motion* is reinforced, plus he learns to get off the bit the moment you take the slack out of the reins, and to back up before the reins come tight, without raising his head or locking his jaw.

You're teaching all this through repeated backing-up instead of repeated stopping. As a result, this is a terrific exercise for improving your horse's stop *without* putting a lot of wear and tear on his hocks. It's also something you can go back to when you begin to add speed if your horse starts to brace, as the Whoa-Back is a great way to soften him up.

Start this exercise at an easy lope. Before you ask for the stop, make sure your horse isn't just "motoring on"; in other words, he should have "at least one ear on you" (meaning he's paying attention). Also, make sure he's traveling straight and "in the box"—not leaning to one side or the other, or pushing on the reins.

If the going gets tough as you're working on your horse's stop (or any time you're working on something your horse finds difficult), remember what I talked about in chapter 2 about riding smart: always go back to the last thing your horse did well, then inch forward again from there. It's normal for the "wheels to come off" (or at least wobble a bit) as you increase speed, as you'll need to do ultimately in your stopping. So if he begins to get pushy, "motors on," or seems confused, fall back to a point where he was "getting it," then proceed even more slowly from there.

Then, remembering all the things you've learned to this point, take a deep breath, sit down, and say "Whoa" (figs. 8.3 A–D). When your horse stops, "back him off your hands" a little more assertively than you have up to this point. To do this, hold your hands softly but firmly at belt level, then bump with both your legs to get him to come off the bit (i.e., you want him to rock back, pick his shoulders up, keep his head down, and stay soft in your hands). If he resists coming off the bit, up the ante by bumping more insistently with both legs in neutral position until he does.

Once he softens, back him up briskly and steadily until he feels as if he's "getting back" (moving his feet more quickly) instead of just backing-up. When he does, release all pressure and let him stand quietly for a moment. Then, without going forward, say "Whoa" again, take the slack out of the reins, and make him "get back" again. At this point, it's important not to pull more or harder to get him to resume backing-up; use your legs as necessary to drive him into the "wall" made by your hands, which then cause him to go back.

When he's backing-up as if he's going somewhere

(other than to a funeral, that is), let him stop and rest again. Keep going like this—backing, then resting—all the way across the arena if need be to get him responding willingly and lightly. Then pick up the lope and start again from the beginning.

Once he's responding willingly at an easy lope, begin to speed him up. Be sure as you do, however, that you also increase his collection by using your legs in neutral position to push him into the bridle. He needs to drive from behind, rather than just "colt lope" on his front end. If he pulls the reins right out of your hands when you ask him to stop, he's falling onto his front end—the result of not enough collection.

### ☞ *Troubleshoot It*

When the horse:

Refuses to stop: Don't jerk on the reins in frustration; instead, pull your horse around on his hocks as I describe in Extra Stopping Help on p. 99.

Falls on his front end or pulls on the reins: Just keep working on this exercise, as it's designed to correct exactly these sorts of problems.

Doesn't lift the shoulders in the backup: Slap his shoulders with both feet at the same time (use the side of the stirrups, not your heel or spurs) as you back. Also, make sure the slack is out of the reins, and use slightly sharper tugs to help lift him up.

Backs up crookedly: See the Shoulder-Swing exercise in the section on backing-up, later in this chapter (see p. 106).

### *"Fencing"*

We used to think "Fencing" (using the fence as a barrier to help get a horse sliding in his stop) made a horse bracy in the front end. But I think we just weren't doing it correctly.

**8.3 A–D** The Whoa-Back

From an easy lope, take a deep breath, sit down, and say "Whoa" (A). Once your horse has stopped and softens to your rein pressure, back him up briskly and steadily until he feels as if he's "getting back" (moving his feet quickly) instead of just backing-up (B). (Don't overuse your reins; think instead in terms of bumping with your legs in neutral position to drive your horse into the "wall" of your hands, which then causes him to back up.) Now release all pressure and let him stand quietly for a moment (C). Then, without going forward, say "Whoa" again, take the slack out of the reins, and make him "get back" again (D).

It depends on the situation. Usually, I "rock my horse back," reinforcing the stop with a "mini backup" by shifting his weight to his rear end and taking a step or two, and then sit for a moment. If he wants to go forward, I definitely don't let him (remember—always do the opposite of what your horse wants to do to reinforce your authority). I make him sit until he's okay staying put, then, I turn 180 degrees and lope off.

If he's content to sit there, I don't mind going straight forward after we've sat for a bit. Finally, if my horse stopped a little "bracy" (stiff and resistant), I might squeeze him forward into the bridle one step at a time, with a little sidepass one way and then the other to soften up his front end.

**8.4** "Fencing"

**Lope a straight line slowly toward the fence, continuing to drive with your legs right up to it until the fence stops your horse. Build speed over time, and as your horse becomes more and more confident, he'll begin to understand how to keep "running" in front as he starts to slide in the back, to keep from colliding with the fence.**

Done properly, Fencing can help teach your horse to run straight and true. This is especially important in a short arena, where your run must be as reasonably long as it can be. If your horse begins to anticipate the upcoming fence and starts to shut down, you'll never get a good stop. Fencing teaches him to keep going toward the fence until you give the signal.

A second reason you Fence is to encourage the horse to drive up underneath himself (push from behind) while giving in the face, raising his shoulders, and rounding his back (in other words, increase his collection—think of that accordion) *without pulling on his face* while sliding. You let the fence do the hard work, and you don't end up the "bad guy."

A third reason for this exercise is to help a horse who's just beginning to slide. Once he's loping straight in his approach to the fence, building speed as his rider dictates (never choosing his own speed), and maintaining that speed as he nears the fence, he'll begin to under-

stand how to keep "running" in front as he starts to slide in the back, to keep from colliding with the fence.

I'll explain how to Fence your horse at a lope; you can also perform it at a trot the first few times.

Begin by loping your horse around for a bit until he's no longer fresh and is beginning to think about wanting to slow down and stop. Then lope a straight line slowly through the middle of the arena toward the end fence (be sure it's a safe one). Use your legs and reins to keep him straight and perpendicular to the fence. Continue to drive with your legs right up to the fence (fig. 8.4). When you reach it, *don't pull on the reins*; let the fence stop your horse. Then stand and rest for a moment, giving your horse a pat. You want the fence to become "a good place to be" in your horse's mind. Then repeat the entire sequence.

As your horse becomes comfortable loping straight up to the fence and stopping, you can begin to say "Whoa" just before the stop.

Over time, as your horse's confidence in this exercise grows, begin to build speed on the approach to the fence. If your horse starts to get nervous, go back to the last speed at which he was completely comfortable, then build even more slowly from there. And, whenever you're stopped at the fence, spend as much time as needed until your horse is calm and relaxed.

The most common mistakes people make with this exercise are failing to continue driving the horse all the way up to the fence, and pulling on the reins instead of letting the fence do the work.

### ☛ Troubleshoot It

When the horse:

"Wiggles" on the approach: If your horse breaks gait or won't stay perpendicular to the fence as he nears it, just continue up to the fence as best you can, then stop and rest. Over time, as your horse comes to understand what's being asked of him, this problem will resolve itself.

Raises his head: If his neck comes up in anticipation of reaching the fence, just continue to drive with your legs in neutral position and bump gently on the reins, as you normally would, to bring his head back down.

Races: If he starts speeding up on his own instead of responding to your cues for speed, just take the slack out of the reins and ask him to soften through the jaw, then draw him down to a trot, then a walk, then a stop, then a backup, all in about six or so strides. Sit there for a while and let him relax. Whatever you do, don't jerk on the reins—this only frightens him and compounds the problem. Remember our discussion of this in the "ride smart" section of chapter 2 (p. 8)—jerking will just make him raise his head and brace through the neck. Another way to deal with it is to change your plan and simply turn at the fence and keep going. Often it's the stop that worries a horse, so by taking the stop away for a bit, he can relax. (In the meantime, you can work on Runarounds, which I describe next.)

After he's relaxed, have another try at the fence.

### The Runaround

The quality of a horse's stop is directly related to the quality of his rundown. This exercise, in which you build to rundown speed, slow, and collect instead of stopping, then go around the end of your arena and build to rundown speed again, is perfect for working on your rundown without the wear and tear of too many stops.

It also helps "take the brace out" of your horse's stop as he learns to "downshift" his weight back on to his hocks to slow down, just as he must when he actually stops. If his first response to being slowed is to drop onto his front end, that's what he'll do when he stops, and that's exactly what you don't want. By *not* stopping, but instead just "downshifting," you can reprogram that response.

The Runaround also helps you develop greater speed in your rundown. Many horses have a low "do-not-exceed speed" (that's the speed you must never go over in an airplane; if you do exceed it and hit turbulence, the wings can fall off!) By pushing your horse up to that speed, backing off and asking him to collect up and soften, then nudging him up to it again, you can desensitize him to going fast. He learns to "stay with you" and continue to respond as you "pour the coal on." Every horse can develop a higher do-not-exceed speed, but some will remain more balanced and in control than others. This exercise helps your horse achieve his best, most controlled rundown speed.

Finally, if you practice the Runaround properly, your horse will naturally begin to slide in his stops. How far he slides will ultimately be determined by his genetics, your feel and timing, the quality of the ground, the nature of his hind sliding plates, and how he feels (i.e., whether or not he's sore). But working on the Runaround will improve the quality of his rundowns, which will naturally improve the quality of his stopping and sliding. In other words, work more on your run, and the stop and slide will take care of itself.

### 8.5 The Runaround

This exercise improves the quality of your horse's rundown, which in turn improves the quality of his stop. Practice this exercise in the middle third of the arena, at least 20 feet from the fence or wall. Simply build speed down the long side of your arena, then sit deep in the saddle and pick up your reins to "downshift" and slow down at the end of the straight as you approach the turn to the short end. Be sure to slow all the way to the speed you wish to ride the short side while still on a straight line—don't let the horse careen around the corner. Keep your horse slow and collected through the short end (using your legs to drive him into the "wall" of your hands), and ask him to gradually build speed again down the next long side. And so on. Work equally in both directions.

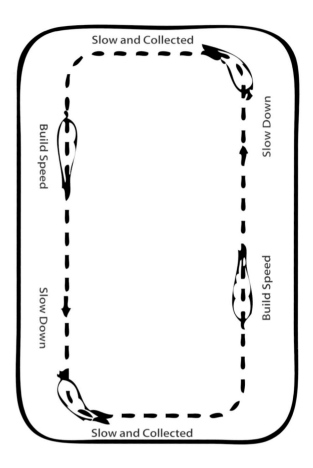

Ride the "build speed" part of the Runaround down the long side of your arena (fig. 8.5). Stay in the middle third of the arena, at least 20 feet in from the fence line so you have room to make corrections, as I discuss in the troubleshooting section below. Ride the slow-collected part around the ends of your arena. As you encourage your horse to build speed, be sure to look up and straight ahead, and keep equal pressure on his sides; this will help him stay straight between your legs and reins. Ride with purpose, so that he keeps one ear on you, indicating he's paying attention. Make sure he's increasing his speed only when you ask him to—not of his own volition.

If he's responding well, ride as if you're going to run all the way to the next ZIP code. Then, as the end of the arena approaches, sit down in the saddle and gather your horse up—think of downshifting an expensive car. Pick up your reins as necessary, but keep your legs slightly closed around him to keep him driving from behind. From all the work you've done to this point, when you pick up the reins he should soften in the jaw and say, "What would you like me to do?"

Keep him soft and collected as you slow down on the straight line at the end of the long side and as you go around the short end, then build speed again down the other long side. Continue on like this until he's doing it well, stop and rest for a bit, then go on. Over time and multiple practice sessions, you'll find he'll be able to reach higher speeds without getting "wobbly in the wheels."

### ☞ Troubleshoot It

When the horse:

Races: If he starts speeding up on his own instead of responding to your cues for speed, break him down to a stop then back up just as described in the solution for racing in the troubleshooting section for Fencing, p. 103.

Leans: If he starts to lean during the build-speed part of the exercise (as toward the barn or gate), draw him

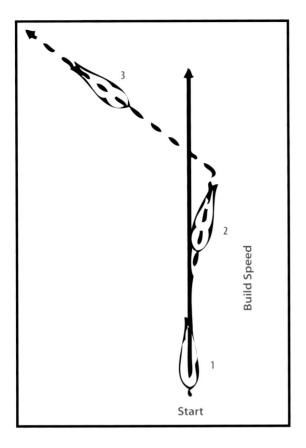

3

Build Speed

2

1

Start

I first explained the benefit of using *overcorrection* to fix potential problems in chapter 6, p. 76. I find this technique is instrumental in keeping your horse on track *anytime* he deviates from an intended straight line. For example, if your horse starts to lean toward a magnet during the "build speed" part of the Runaround (2), simply change course by 30 degrees (in the direction opposite of his lean), and continue on that new line, improvising until you can get back on the track of your Runaround (3). (Note: practicing the Runaround in the middle third of the arena gives you room for overcorrective action in either direction.) This sort of "healthy confusion" is useful to keep your horse paying attention to your cues.

back and change course about 30 degrees to overcorrect the lean, then continue on that line (fig. 8.6). If he leans again, make another 30-degree correction, and so on. If you wind up going in the opposite direction altogether, that's okay—it's the sort of "healthy confusion" that keeps your horse guessing and therefore paying attention to you. As you can, pick up the track of your Runaround again, and keep going.

Drops a shoulder/falls out of a lead: This commonly happens when you ask for the slowdown, if your horse doesn't engage both hocks equally. To correct it, don't make a big fuss, but in the space of about six strides, softly draw him to you and break him to a trot, then a walk, then "Whoa," then back him up for a bit and ask him to soften his jaw to the reins. Resume the exercise, but this time, before asking him to slow down, make sure you've softened him in the face (gentle bumping

on the reins if need be) before applying your off-lead leg (i.e., if he's on the left lead, use your right leg) just behind neutral position to drive him up so he can't fall out of the lead.

## Backing-Up

The most impressive backup is straight and speedy. Some horses can almost trot backward, an impressive achievement that is rewarded by a judge for its higher degree of difficulty. Even so, especially in the beginning, you're better off aiming just to get your horse to round his back, tuck his head in, stay soft in his jaw, and step smartly straight back 10 to 20 feet—*without* amazing speed (figs. 8.7 A & B).

If you push for too much speed, you run the risk of your horse rolling back, veering off track, or even tripping and falling down.

In addition to being an essential part of the rundown/stop/backup maneuver, backing-up is important as a schooling tool. That's because what backing-up requires of your horse is similar to what stopping requires of him (as I discussed in teaching the Whoa-Back, p. 99). Moreover, the correction for a poor stop

**8.7 A & B** Contact when backing-up

The most impressive backup is straight and speedy, but don't aim for speed too soon. Instead, work to get your horse to round his back, tuck his head, stay soft in his jaw, and step smartly straight back 10 to 12 feet. This will initially require firm contact with his mouth as you give him the backup cue while bumping with your legs (A). With practice and work on the Whoa-Back, your horse will learn to stay soft and start backing-up when you simply pick up the reins, *before* you make contact with his mouth (B). He should continue to back up until you stop asking him to—by sitting quietly with your legs relaxed and no pressure on the reins.

is often backing-up. So to be effective when training your horse to stay soft in the face and to stop well, you must teach him to back up fluidly while off the bit and remaining straight (i.e., both hocks are equally engaged and both shoulders are equally elevated).

In this section, I review what you already know about backing-up, then I'll give you an exercise, the Shoulder-Swing, designed to increase your control over your horse's shoulders—the key to keeping him straight.

In Essential 4: Backing-Up (p. 54), you taught your horse to back up in response to pressure on the bit. At that point, if he backed crookedly, you simply moved his hind end back over to the line you were backing on. In the Whoa-Back exercise earlier in this chapter (p. 99), you worked on softening your horse so he can become resistance-free in his backup, and making him "get back"—that is, move his feet more quickly.

To back up well enough for competition, your horse must be perfectly straight *and* reasonably speedy. To achieve this, you'll need to gain more and better control

of his shoulders, because if he's not traveling straight and smartly, that's likely where the problem lies.

Remember, when trying to get a correct maneuver of any sort most of the problems you encounter trace to your horse's shoulders. It's one of the primary ways he "gets" us! To counteract this, you must maintain total control of his shoulders, so he can't keep that particular resistance in his bag of tricks. And, one of the best ways to gain shoulder control is through work in the backup. Once you do gain precise control of his shoulders, you'll not only polish your backup, you'll also be able to improve most other maneuvers, as well.

To gain shoulder control, you need to learn the Shoulder-Swing.

### Shoulder-Swing

In this exercise, whenever your horse's hind end veers off course in the backup, instead of moving it back over, swing his shoulders over 90 degrees to reestablish the straight line before resuming backing-up (fig. 8.8). This activates his shoulders, so that he begins picking them up more freely and evenly, which will enable him to back up straight.

Begin by picking up your reins, taking the slack out *evenly*, and asking him to back up. Don't anticipate his going crooked and try to keep him straight; just ask correctly and then let him perform. If his hind end does swing off track, it likely will be to the right—once again, because of that natural asymmetry I talked about in chapter 2, p. 18. So, you need to bring his shoulders over to the right to straighten him.

Do this by bringing both reins toward the belt loop on your right side. At the same time, slap your horse's left shoulder with your left foot (not your spur!) to reinforce the lateral movement. Try to get him to move his shoulders over crisply off your left rein, and keep them moving for a full 90 degrees, then release. Pick up your reins again and ask him to resume backing. It's important that you release completely and pick up your reins in a new unit of time so you give the horse the opportunity to "stand his shoulders up" equally and back up correctly in response to the slack being taken out of the reins.

If you feel that his shoulders aren't picking up evenly (and you'll likely notice from the first step if they aren't), you'll find that he gets crooked again. If so, repeat the Shoulder-Swing to straighten him, then ask him to back up again. Continue like this until he backs up straight and goes faster (and still straight) when you "cluck" rhythmically for cadence and speed. (I find it helps to provide an audible cue for establishing rhythm.) It may take a while, so be patient.

Once you've taught him this exercise, be sure to stay after him *every* time you back up until he responds automatically to pick his shoulders up, get off the bit, and back up straight and cadenced. You'll be amazed at how it feels when he really does begin to get it-light and "steppy," with no resistance anywhere.

Note: a little of the Shoulder-Swing correction goes a long way, so don't overdo it. In particular, as you get

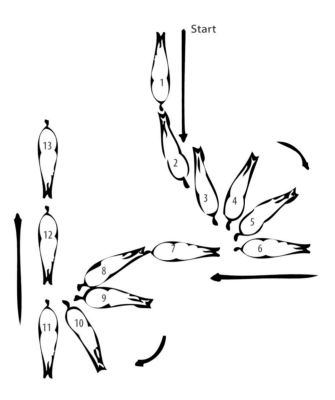

**8.8** The Shoulder-Swing
**Use this exercise when your horse's hind end veers off course in the backup. Instead of moving his hind end back over, swing his shoulders over 90 degrees in the direction his hind end is veering to reestablish the straight line, then resume backing-up in the new direction.**

close to show time, avoid it so he doesn't get confused and start thinking you want him to roll back when he's backing-up (see lessons on rollbacks below).

The Shoulder-Swing will help you perfect your backup. Now, let's move to the rollback.

## Rolling Back

A good rollback is a fluid motion. The horse slides in his stop as far as momentum will take him, hesitates for a split second, then turns 180 degrees by dramatically "cracking back over his hocks" and swinging his forehand around. He then lopes off (on the correct lead) out of the same tracks he stopped in.

It used to be that a "lope around" was acceptable in a reining class. That was where, instead of a true rollback, the horse made a small arc to accomplish a 180-degree change of direction. But now, to score well, your horse must "use himself," working his body intensely as he "turns inside out," coming out of the rollback on the correct lead and—in contrast—casually loping off in the new direction. On a loose rein! If you can do this, you'll significantly add to the score of your rundown/ stop/rollback, which is scored as a single unit.

As important as the rollback is, it's one of the least practiced parts of a pattern. That's because if you practice stopping and rolling back too often, your horse will begin anticipating the rollback with a lean in the direction he thinks he will turn during the stop, which causes him to stop crookedly.

You can avoid this leaning problem by backing-up before performing a slow rollback in practice. If you're Fencing, you can also stop into the fence, slowly turn 180 degrees away from the fence, then sit quietly for a bit. Both these maneuvers avoid the problem of anticipation while getting your horse comfortable with the basic concept of rollbacks.

In this section, I'm going to explain how to develop and refine your horse's rollback. But first, I'll give you an exercise called Come-Around that serves as preparation for the rollback.

### Come-Around

The purpose of this exercise is simply to make sure your horse understands that when you draw both reins back, with the direct rein straight back toward your outer belt loop and the indirect rein steadying with backward pressure toward your midline, you want him to "load up on his hind end" and come right around on his hocks.

This maneuver is essentially a "more broke" version of the Doubling you learned in chapter 5 (see p. 46). You can now do it on or off the fence, but either way you want your horse to "find" his hocks and come around, soft to your hands, when you pull on the reins (figs. 8.9 A–D).

Start at the walk. When your horse is moving ahead freely and rhythmically, draw the direct rein (let's say your left) up and back toward the outer belt loop on that side. Keep enough backward pressure on the right rein to balance him, bumping it softly if necessary to soften his jaw. Also use right leg pressure at the cinch. This should cause your horse to come around, ideally using his inside (left) hind leg to pivot on, though you needn't worry overly about that at first—it'll come.

When he can do it reliably in both directions, proceed to the trot, and then the lope.

When he can consistently perform the Come-Around on his hind end at the lope (and of course he already knows about stopping on "Whoa"), you're ready to try an actual rollback.

### The Rollback

The key thing here is to make this maneuver *no big deal*—you want your horse to think of it simply as an extension of the stop, but with a change of direction. So, for starters, you're going to stop, back up a few steps, and then roll back into the fence, turning 270 degrees and not just 180, without rushing (figs. 8.10 A–H). (At a show, the backup portion will be shortened to a simple rock-back—see p. 99—but for now a few steps is ideal.)

Pick up a lope on the correct lead (i.e., if the fence is on your right, you're on the left lead). Continue until your horse is loping easily and relaxed, and you're sitting up evenly with your shoulders back, breathing deeply. Then, traveling down the long side of the arena, about 10 feet away from the fence, take a deep breath, sit down, exhale, and say "Whoa." (As always, don't lean back or pull back on the reins, or your horse will brace against you and become hollow.)

Once your horse has stopped, pick up your reins and ask him to back up a few steps; keep your rein pressure the same so he lifts both shoulders evenly and travels straight back. On the last step or two, apply slightly more

**8.9 A–D** The Come-Around

This exercise is a "more broke" version of Doubling (see p. 46). You can perform it on the fence, as I am here, or off it. Start with pressure from both legs in neutral position to move your horse straight forward, freely and rhythmically, then draw the direct rein up and back toward the belt loop on the turn-side (A & B).

At the same time, maintain enough backward pressure on the indirect rein to balance your horse, bumping softly if necessary to soften his jaw. Also use pressure at the cinch (here, from my right leg) to drive his front end around (C). When he's completed coming around, use both legs in neutral position to drive him straight forward in the opposite direction (D).

**8.10 A–H** The rollback with backup

In the beginning, insert a few steps of backup into your stop/ rollback sequence. To do this, bring your horse to a stop, then pick up your reins and ask him to back a few steps, keeping your rein pressure equal so he lifts both shoulders evenly and travels straight back (A & B). On the last step or two, apply slightly more pressure to the rein on the side of the intended rollback (the direct rein) to tip your horse's nose in that direction (C & D). Look in the direction you're going, and carry both your hands toward your side

G

H

belt loop (your inside hand may even come as high as your armpit, as mine is here). This keeps your horse working off his hocks. Continue around like this, using your outside leg (my left leg) at the cinch to help move your horse's front end (E & F). Note that I'm go-ing round more than 180 degrees; for this exercise, 270 degrees is better. As you prepare to lope away, use plenty of that same leg (my left), moved back a bit, to encourage your horse to pick up the correct (in this case, right) lead. And off you go (G & H)!

pressure to the direct rein to tip his nose slightly in the direction you want to go (toward the fence). As you do this, look in that direction, as well, and carry both your hands toward your fence-side belt loop (avoid dropping your indirect rein hand onto your horse's neck). Don't lean toward the fence or pull your direct rein hand way out, or your horse will go shoulder first instead of working off his hocks. And, don't pull down with the reins or you'll just pull your horse onto his front end.

If you cue him properly, your horse should stay rocked back on his hind end as he rolls back into the fence. At that point, keep your cues in place and his nose tipped in the direction of movement until he comes around 270 degrees and is facing more toward the center of the arena. Release your cues and sit quietly for a moment, lope off, and use plenty of outside leg behind neutral position to make sure he picks up the correct lead.

Once he's consistently rolling back like this in both directions along the fence, try it out in the open. When he's good at stopping/backing-up/rolling-back in the open, return to the fence, only now change the sequence to: stop, rock back, turn at least 180 degrees (270 degrees is even better), and lope off *without hesitating* (figs. 8.11 A–C).

To accomplish this, begin to use what will be your new outside leg *as soon as your horse is committed to the rollback*, so that he's prepared to lope straightaway on the correct lead. In other words, as your horse is starting to turn into the fence to the right, begin to use your left leg just behind neutral position to ask for the right lead halfway through the rollback.

### ☞ Troubleshoot It

When the horse:

Turns too soon: This is when a horse tries to begin the rollback before he gets to the "bottom" of his stop, and it is why we do a short backup first, later shortening it to a rock-back only. If you start to have problems with

this after you've gone to using the rock-back, return to a few backup steps for a while until the horse stops anticipating. Also try turning the opposite way from what your horse is expecting.

Leads with the shoulder: If your horse doesn't back up straight and consequently leads the turn with his shoulder, catch him at the end of the 180 and back him up again, straight. Pull evenly on both reins to start the backup, then use the "key in the ignition" twist of the wrist (and pressure from the same-side leg) to get the offending shoulder "standing up" properly. Then turn another 180 in the same direction. Keep doing this until he steps around the 180 degrees balanced and straight in his body.

Gets stuck in backup mode: It's especially easy for this to happen after your horse is in the bridle (see p. 126) and you're riding one-handed—he just keeps backing-up and refuses to turn. To fix it, pull the direct rein (the rein on the side you're turning into) a bit wider while keeping pressure on the indirect rein and just wait him out. When he does turn, reward him, let him rest a moment, then try it again to reinforce his understanding. (I discuss riding one-handed in chapter 10.)

Lunges through the turn (usually shoulder first): Back up very straight before the turn, taking care to get that shoulder on the side you're going to turn into up and out of the way *before* you let him turn. If you're turning to the right, pull your left rein out to the left a bit to pull your horse's shoulders that way, while picking up the right shoulder by twisting your right hand in the "key in the ignition" move. Then apply backward pressure to both reins while your hands are in this position. Don't let your horse rush through it—make him step with balance. Be sure, too, that you also use the direct rein to guide his nose into the turn first. If he beats you into the turn with his head going the wrong way, catch

**8.11 A–C** The rollback without backup

Eventually, you can eliminate the backup steps. Instead, allow your horse to slide in his stop as far as momentum will take him, hesitate for a split second as you rock him back, then look in the direction you're turning, use your inside (direct) rein to tip his nose in the direction of the rollback, and carry both your hands toward your side belt loop (A & B). Once he's committed to the turn, use your outside leg (here, my left leg) at the cinch to drive his shoulders around. As he comes through the 180-degree turn, keep using the same leg (again, my left) a bit farther back to ask for the correct (right) lead as he lopes off (C).

him after the rollback and pull him softly into a spin in the same direction until you get his nose tipped to the inside and he's following it around willingly.

Rolls "around" instead of rolling back: Your horse loses his balance and "falls off" his hind end, falling out of the rollback after going only 90 degrees, and doesn't exit in the tracks he made coming in to the stop. Again, catch him at the end of the turn, rock him back onto his hind end, and turn him the same way again, slowing it down a tad and being sure he gets all the way around at least 270 degrees on his hind end.

Quits before the full 180 degrees: Rock him back on his hocks and go again, only try to go 270 degrees this time—and every time for a while.

## Exercise: Mixing It Up

As you work on refining your horse's stop, backup, and rollback, don't follow the same sequences repeatedly or your horse will begin to anticipate what comes next. When this happens, he'll beat you to it by dropping his shoulder (the "easier" way for him), instead of balanced over his hind end, the way you want.

So, to avoid this anticipation, create the "healthy confusion" that keeps him waiting and listening to you for direction (see p. 99). Do this by constantly changing the order of maneuvers and where you do them in the arena.

Also, choose a different spot to stop at each time. After the stop, sometimes back up only; other times back up or rock back and then roll back. Whatever you think your horse is expecting, do the opposite.

When you do roll back, sometimes roll left, sometimes roll right. Again, try to sense which way your horse *thinks* you want to go, then go the other way.

Be creative, but don't make any one practice session overly long. If you do, your horse may get tired or bored, and quit trying to stop completely each time, especially if you've been practicing a lot of rollbacks. When this happens, resist the temptation to simply pull the reins harder to force him to stop. Instead, go back to that abrupt turn into the fence, remembering to pull the direct rein up toward your side belt loop. This is hard work for him and reminds him to start trying again. Follow this with just backing-up plus the 180 degree turn a few times, then quit work for the day.

# 9 LEAD CHANGES

N ot "getting changed" is the most expensive penalty levied in the reining pattern in competition. At the same time, earning credit points for the flying change is one of the most difficult things to do. (A *flying* change is when you switch leads at the lope; a *simple* change is when you come down to a trot or walk before picking up the new lead.) Part of the reason a change can be so problematic is that it's the maneuver horses anticipate most.

But—not to worry! In this chapter, I set you up to succeed by achieving your changes. First, I give you two exercises—the Turn on the Forehand and the Counter-Canter—to prepare you and your horse to do flying changes. Second, I explain exactly how I want you to accomplish a lead change, and provide some tips for dealing with the problems you're most likely to run into in the troubleshooting section.

Finally, I talk about two exercises—the Daisy and Two-Tracking—that will help you work toward perfecting your changes, and include troubleshooting tips for those exercises, too.

Before I begin, bear in mind that the quality of your lead *departure* will have much to do with the quality of your lead *change*. I talked about lead departures in chapter 7 in preparation for riding circles (see p. 81). You may want to go back and review that material before beginning work on flying changes.

## Preparing to Change

To prepare to do flawless flying lead changes, work on the Turn on the Forehand and Counter-Cantering.

### Turn on the Forehand

In this maneuver, your horse's front end stays put while you push his hind end around in a 360-degree circle. It reinforces your control over your horse's hind end separately from his shoulders—that is, though his hind end moves, his shoulders don't, which will give you an extra tool to use if your horse doesn't want to change his lead.

Your horse must be soft in the face and move well off your leg to accomplish this maneuver.

To do a Turn on the Forehand to the right, use your

right (direct) rein to tip your horse's nose slightly to the right (figs. 9.1 A–D). At the same time, use the "key in the ignition" move with the right rein (rotating your wrist clockwise) to "pick up" his right shoulder and keep it from moving right as you press just behind neutral position with your left leg, pushing his hindquarters around. Ask for just one step at a time.

Be sure his front end doesn't also move to the right; if need be hold your right rein up against his neck and use your right leg right at or a bit in front of the cinch. Also, don't let him push forward into the bridle; if he tries to, hold or bump gently on both reins to get him off the bit.

Be sure to work equally in both directions until your horse is fluid and responsive either way. This is only your second time working on "separating" the front end from the back end (lead departures were the first). It's difficult and confusing for your horse. Be patient but persistent.

### Counter-Canter

A Counter-Canter is simply loping on the wrong lead, on purpose. Why would you want to do this? Because anytime you find something that's hard for a horse to do, you're onto something useful. Counter-Cantering requires discipline, and accomplishing it will help supple your horse, strengthen a new set of muscles, and enhance his ambidexterity and balance. It also fine-tunes your control of his shoulders.

More importantly, Counter-Cantering ultimately encourages your horse to change his lead. He'll find Counter-Cantering challenging, so you can use it to set him up to volunteer to do the "easier" thing, which is to change.

Counter-Canter also gives you a tool to use when your horse begins anticipating a lead change. For example, you can set him up for a lead change as you come across the center of the arena, then *not* change and simply Counter-Canter into the new circle. In this

way, he learns to wait for you and change only in response to your cues.

When you first attempt the Counter-Canter, do it in a big field or large arena, where you have plenty of room to maneuver without having to make tight turns or smallish circles, which would tempt your horse to change instead of continue in the Counter-Canter.

Start by walking a few steps in the "lead-departure frame" (see p. 80), then lope, picking up the correct lead. Gradually straighten out your trajectory and begin to curve around in the other direction so that you're traveling a large circle on the "wrong" lead—a Counter-Canter. As you're about to go in the "wrong" direction, keep your horse soft with pressure from your inside leg ("inside" meaning the inside of the new circle) at or just behind neutral position; this supports the lead he's on. At the same time, hold up his inside shoulder with the "key in the ignition" on the inside rein so he doesn't dive into the new direction and change leads on you. Then try to get as many strides in Counter-Canter as you can, gradually asking for more.

If your horse does change just as the Counter-Canter is to begin, be patient; he's responding to a loss in balance caused by dropping his shoulder, which makes diving onto the correct lead the easiest thing to do. Give him time to understand what you're asking—to stay on what feels to him like the "wrong" lead. If he does try to change at this point, chances are he'll only change in front (i.e., with his front legs but not his hind), so break down to a walk and start again.

At first, as you Counter-Canter, tip your horse's nose to the inside—in the direction of the circle (fig. 9.2). This teaches him to hold his balance by keeping his inside shoulder up. It also helps him learn to change direction by shifting his weight to his hocks, instead of falling on his front end and dropping his shoulder.

As his balance improves, work more on softening his face and staying on a true, symmetric circle, all the while keeping his inside shoulder up and his nose

**9.1 A–D** The Turn on the Forehand

A Turn on the Forehand (where your horse's front end stays put while you push his hind end around in a circle) prepares your horse for lead changes because it gives you control of the hind end. To do a Turn on the Forehand to the right (so your horse's hind end is moving to your right), use your right (direct) rein to tip his nose slightly to the right, steadying with your left (indirect) rein so his nose doesn't tip too far (A). At the same time, also use the "key in the ignition" move with your right rein (rotating your wrist clockwise) to pick up your horse's right shoulder and keep it from moving right as you simultaneously press just behind neutral position with your left leg, pushing his hindquarters around (B & C). Ask for just one step at a time, making sure his front end doesn't also move to the right. Here, my horse has completed almost 180 degrees with his hind end (D); keep cueing in the same fashion until your horse completes a full 360-degree circle with his hindquarters. Note how I'm keeping my horse's nose tipped as we go. Remember too, as always, to work equally in both directions.

**9.2** Counter-Canter (head in)

A Counter-Canter (loping on the "wrong" lead on purpose) will set your horse up to *want* to change leads. Here, my horse is on the right lead while circling to the left. Begin Counter-Cantering with your horse's head tipped in the direction of the circle, as I am here. Use "key in the ignition" pressure on the inside (direct) rein to keep him from diving in and changing leads. At the same time, apply soft pressure at or just behind neutral position with your inside leg (here, my left leg) to keep him soft through his body.

**9.3** Counter-Canter (head out)

As your horse gets better at Counter-Cantering, begin to bring his nose to the outside of the circle. Here, my horse is still on the right lead, circling to the left, only now his head is tipped just a bit to the outside of the circle. To accomplish this, carry both reins toward the inside of the circle, but bring your indirect rein (here, my right rein) a bit back toward your belly button and against his neck. Also bump with your outside leg (here, my right leg) in neutral position to keep him on the same circle without changing leads.

tipped to the inside. Do this by using your inside leg at neutral position and lifting his inside shoulder with your hand, while using your outside leg behind neutral so his rear end stays on the circle. Because your horse's inside front leg isn't the lead leg, there's nothing in the way of getting his head lower. So work on that, as well.

Gradually begin to make your circles smaller, too, which will be more challenging for your horse.

As your horse gets better at the Counter-Canter, begin to bring his nose to the *outside*, so that he's Counter-Cantering with it tipped to the outside of the circle (fig. 9.3). You'll notice that if you don't simultaneously move his shoulders in, you won't be able to stay on the same circle. So, carry both reins toward the inside of the

circle, but bring your outside rein a bit back toward your belly button and against his neck. Also bump with your outside leg in neutral position to keep him on the same circle without changing leads. This will work on a whole different set of body parts, and is equally as important as working with his nose tipped to the inside.

When your horse can lope as comfortably on the counter lead as on the correct one—that is, when he's become ambidextrous—you're ready to move on to lead changes.

## Flying Changes

Changing leads is one of the few reining maneuvers a horse does at liberty, on his own. Horses don't slide, spin, or back up when they're loose, but they change leads all day long. However, when *we* ask our horses to change a lead, a lot of things happen in a very short time. Horses start to anticipate these cues, making a lead change the hardest maneuver to keep pure.

Because changes are challenging, set yourself up for success before you attempt them by making sure your horse is soft in the face and in response to rein pressure, moves laterally in both directions off your leg, and can Counter-Canter well. When you do, changing leads will not be such "a big deal" to your horse. This is critically important, because it's much easier to keep lead changes low-key if they never become an anxiety-producing, frustrating experience in your horse's mind.

There are various ways to teach a horse to change his lead; I'm going to show you a simple method of "tricking" him into changing to make it relatively easy for him. This enables him to learn the basics of what you want in a non-stressful way. As mentioned, I'll give you two exercises—the Daisy and the Two-Track—to help you refine the "trick" into a reliable cue-and-response, with little or no anxiety, or anticipation on your horse's part.

Think of changing leads as going from a departure on one lead to a departure on the other lead—*while loping*. Begin by loping a Counter-Canter circle in your arena, keeping your horse's nose and rear end tipped to the inside of the circle (figs. 9.4 A & B). As you approach a corner, carry both hands to the outside to move his shoulders out toward the arena fence. (As you do, keep enough pressure on the inside rein to keep his nose tipped to the inside.) At the same time, take your inside leg off for a stride and gradually start to apply pressure with your outside leg, a little behind neutral position, and "kiss" just as you go into the corner. If he doesn't change at that point, bump more aggressively with your outside leg and "kiss" again.

He may try to take the impulsion you're creating with your outside leg and simply go faster. If that starts to happen, "set him down" in the corner by pulling

**9.4 A & B** Flying changes

**To make a flying lead change easy in the beginning, lope a Counter-Canter circle. (Here my horse is on the right lead in a circle to the left.) As you approach a corner of your arena, carry both hands to the outside to move your horse's shoulders out toward the fence, keeping enough pressure on the inside (direct) rein to keep his nose tipped to the inside. At the same time, take your inside leg (my left leg) off for a stride and gradually start to apply pressure with your outside leg, a little behind neutral position (A). Then, just as you go into the corner, make a "kiss" sound (I use this vocal cue to help "lift" the horse into the change). If your horse doesn't change at that point, bump more aggressively with your outside leg (behind neutral) and "kiss" again. Here my horse is complying by changing onto his left lead (B).**

on your reins assertively enough to get him stopped right away, but without jerking. The reason he didn't change was because he didn't move his rear end away from your leg. Remind him how to do this by walking in "lead-departure frame" into a correct-lead lope (see p. 80), or doing a quick Turn on the Forehand (as I described in the beginning of this chapter). Then just put him back into Counter-Canter and try again—no big deal.

He's going to *want* to change, as loping on the wrong lead is harder and not as natural for him as loping on the correct one. Still, sometimes it takes a little time for him to "get it." Just be patient, don't get flustered, and keep asking.

As soon as he does change on cue, let him lope an easy three or four strides, then gently break him down to a walk. (Gently stopping, rather than barreling along in the new lead, will keep him from getting pushy. I'd rather have to encourage my horse to keep loping after a change than have to struggle to hold him in.)

Once he's stopped, sit a moment and praise him lavishly. Remember from chapter 2: you want him to think, "Hey, I'm pretty darn good at changing leads—it's easy for me!" not "Omigosh, changing leads is trouble with a capital 'T'—I just can't do it!"

When you've got a change going one way, try to establish one going the other direction. Then quit for the day. This method, again, is just a little "trick" that helps your horse "get it." Once he does, changing becomes easier, but he must then learn to do it anytime, anywhere, on command. Then the real problems can potentially arise, *as he begins to anticipate*. (But that's what the exercises to come will help you avoid!) In the meantime, try to keep his anxiety level down and the initial sessions as low-key as possible.

When your horse gets the idea of how to change in the corner, you can begin asking for changes at different places in the arena, away from the arena fence. Try always to set him up with his body straight, and his shoulders up, before asking for the change. If you're on the left lead before the change, use your right rein and right leg in neutral position to straighten his body, and when you switch to using your left leg (behind neutral) to ask for the change, keep holding that right shoulder up, so he doesn't go to the right immediately.

After he's gone several strides on the new lead (but in the same direction), with his shoulder up and his nose tipped in the new direction (but not going that way yet!), *then* let him go in the new direction, as long as he stays balanced and "with you" (i.e., not pushing into the bridle to go faster).

This part about timing and new direction of travel is critically important, because you should never, *ever* let your horse change direction the moment he changes leads. If you do, he will quickly form a habit of dropping his shoulder toward the new direction, prompting him to change only in front and causing you to lose control of his body. If he tries to change direction *as* he changes leads, just keep going in the original direction, Counter-Cantering on the new lead, and do this consistently until he stops trying to change course on his own.

### ☞ Troubleshoot It

When the horse:

Gets pushy or rushes: If this happens before, during, or after a lead change, break down to a stop and do a Turn on the Forehand as you learned earlier in this chapter (see p. 115). If you were asking for a change to the right lead, you need to sharpen his response to your left leg, so do a Turn on the Forehand to the right, using your left leg behind neutral position to push his hind end counter-clockwise around his forehand. As you do, be sure your horse's nose is tipped to the right (i.e., in the same direction his rear end is going), so his shoulder can't move along with his rear end. All the while, use a sensitive feel of the reins to keep your horse flexed at the poll and soft in the face.

Anticipates: Keep loping around without asking for a change until he stops "looking for it." Always vary where you do ask, and once you graduate from asking only in the corner, don't begin asking only in the center of the pen. Mix it up in terms of what you ask for (a change, no change, a Counter-Canter in the same direction, Counter-Canter in a new direction), as well. (More on this when I discuss the Daisy exercise, below.)

Refuses to change: Whatever you do, don't make a big deal of it if your horse resists your cues. If he didn't change, it's because he didn't move his rear end in response to your outside leg pressure. So, simply stop and do a Turn on the Forehand, as described earlier in this chapter, to remind him how to move off your leg. Next, ask for a change again in a different corner of the arena. Note: I don't advocate doing a simple lead change (breaking down to a trot and then picking up the lope again on the new lead) as preparation for a flying change. It doesn't usually help a horse learn to lift his shoulders and change the way you need him to. A lot of people use a single pole on the ground at the point where you'll ask for the change; it helps a horse to lift up and change leads as he goes over it. This isn't a bad idea if you continue to have difficulty getting the change.

## Exercises: Daisy and Two-Tracking

These two exercises give you plenty of opportunity to work on lead changes while preventing the horse from anticipating them. I describe each exercise, then provide troubleshooting information for both.

### *Daisy*

You already did this exercise earlier, as part of the work on collection and steering in chapter 6 (see p. 73). So take a moment to review the information before proceeding to use the Daisy in two new ways, riding it at the lope:

1 Change leads as you come through the center of the "daisy," continue traveling straight to the end of the "petal," then turn in the new direction and head back to the center.

2 Set up for a change through the center by straightening out your horse's body with your outside rein and leg, but *do not* change. Instead, continue around the end of the "petal," turning in the same direction. This teaches your horse not to anticipate and change on his own.

By mixing it up (sometimes changing leads, often not changing), you create the "healthy confusion" I've discussed before that requires your horse to wait until you tell him what to do.

Below I explain how to ask for the change while on a left lead, changing to the right lead; simply reverse all the cues to accomplish a right-to-left change. As you work, strive to keep your horse quiet, soft, and balanced.

Pick up a left lead (make sure it's a good departure). Go to the end of the "petal" and, with your horse's nose tipped slightly to the left, turn to the left to head back toward the center of the "daisy." As you go around this turn, start using your right rein toward your belly button with your right leg at or just behind the cinch to straighten out your horse's body.

But, instead of riding him on a straight line as you did in chapter 6, keep tension on the right rein to keep his right shoulder up, and his nose tipped the slightest bit to the right.

When you get to the center, take your right leg off your horse's side, go one stride, then press with your left leg behind neutral position and "kiss" if necessary to ask for the change. Use your right rein to keep the horse from going to the right (that "key in the ignition" again), and continue straight to the end of the next "petal." Only then turn to the right, on the new lead.

Keep the horse's nose slightly tipped to the right and, as you start to come out of the turn and head

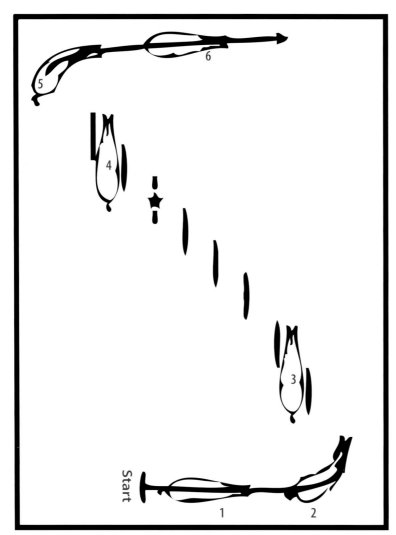

Going forward and laterally across the arena is a great exercise for practicing lead changes. As you come around the corner at 5 o'clock (2), use your right rein and leg (in neutral position) to straighten your horse out, then start to push him diagonally across the arena with assertive pressure from your right leg at or just behind the cinch, while using your right (indirect) rein as need be to keep him from turning and simply loping across the diagonal (3). When you get two-thirds of the way across the diagonal (star), ask for a lead change by taking your right leg off for a stride, then applying your left leg behind neutral and "kissing" (I use this vocal cue to help "lift" my horse into the lead change), then continuing on the same diagonal track after the change until you reach the arena fence (5 & 6). Never allow the horse to change direction when he changes leads. Also, don't change every time; sometimes Counter-Canter in the new direction to avoid anticipation. Reverse cues to go the opposite way.

back toward the middle, begin bringing tension into your left rein, moving your hand toward your belly button, and applying pressure with your left leg in neutral position to straighten him out. Start to tip his nose slightly left to straighten him, and as you do so he may anticipate a change of lead. If he does, just hold him like that, don't change, and go to the end of a "petal," where you can turn to the right or Counter-Canter to the left.

Do as many variations on this theme as you can to keep your horse waiting for *you* to call the shots. And remember: quiet, soft, balanced.

## Two-Tracking

You learned to Two-Track (or leg-yield) at the lope in the Essential 6: Moving Off Your Leg (p. 59). You moved diagonally from one corner of the arena to the other, your horse moving forward and laterally at the same time.

You'll now add on to that by (sometimes!) asking for a change of lead along that diagonal line (fig. 9.5). I explain how to do it starting on the left lead; just reverse all cues to start on the right lead.

Traveling on the rail, ask for a good lope departure onto the left lead. Think of your arena as the face of a

## ▪ Backing-in-a-Circle to Fix Lead-Change "Diving" ▪

This exercise is a variation on the one you learned in chapter 7 to correct cutting in on a circle (see p. 86). Here, use it to correct your horse when he drops his shoulder and "dives" into the new direction after a lead change: bring him to a stop, then back him up in a circle.

Because this form of backing-up is hard work for your horse, it really makes him think twice about dropping that shoulder in the first place. It also makes him more supple and quiet-minded—a perfect training combination.

Here's how to do it. The moment you feel your horse dropping a shoulder and diving into the new direction after a lead change, gently break him down to a stop. Put him in reverse and back him up on a circle (going counterclockwise if he dove to the right after a change to the right lead, or going clockwise if he dove to the left after a change to the left lead). To back him up on a circle:

▸ Tip your horse's nose to the inside (using the direct rein with lifting pressure—remember that "key in the ignition" twist of your wrist).

▸ Pull his shoulders to the outside and "stand them up straight" by carrying both your hands slightly to the outside, with backward pressure.

▸ Keep his hind end to the inside by bumping with your outside leg behind neutral position.

If this is too challenging, break it up. Back up two steps, then push his rear end in for two steps, back up two steps, then move his shoulders out for two steps, and so on. Eventually, just string it all together.

All this requires serious concentration and coordination on the part of both you and your horse. Once you've perfected it, though, this exercise will give you control of his shoulders in a way no other exercise can. Use it whenever your horse tries to dive in a new direction after a lead change.

---

clock: as you come counterclockwise around on the rail to 5 o'clock, begin a Two-Track across the diagonal to 11 o'clock. In other words, as you come around that corner at 5 o'clock, use your right rein and leg (in neutral position) to straighten your horse out, then start to push him diagonally across the arena. Do this with assertive pressure from your right leg at or just behind the cinch, while using your right rein as need be to keep him from turning and simply loping across the diagonal.

Be sure to keep his body perpendicular to the short ends of the arena (or parallel with the long sides—think of it however it is easiest for you to remember). Your horse's nose can be tipped slightly to the right as you go across, though ultimately you'll want it tipped

slightly to the left, in the direction you're traveling. Don't let him lead with his shoulders; really make him step across himself—in other words, he should be traveling about one part forward for every one part across.

When you get two-thirds of the way across the diagonal toward 11 o'clock, take your right leg off for a stride, then apply your left leg behind neutral, with a "kiss" if necessary, while keeping both reins moving and pulling his shoulders toward the left (in other words, you're taking his shoulder *away* from the lead change). What you want is for his body to actually keep going diagonally left even after he's changed to the right lead (all your work with Counter-Cantering will make this doable). He should follow the exact same path he was on, until he gets to 11 o'clock at the wall. Then, with his nose tipped to the right, go through the corner to the right, on the correct lead.

Then reverse all cues to accomplish the same thing from the right lead, starting the diagonal line at 1 o'clock and going laterally across to 7 o'clock.

Don't change every time you come across the diagonal, or of course your horse will begin to antici-pate it. Mix it up so that "healthy confusion" keeps your horse listening to you. Whenever you *are* planning to change, if you feel your horse begin to anticipate the change at the two-thirds point, change your plan and *don't* change; simply Counter-Canter around the cor-ner and go around the arena to try again later.

### ☞ Troubleshoot It

When the horse:

Gets strong or pushes through the bridle: If your horse begins to rush or pull on you, "set him down" by sitting down in the saddle, with your shoulders square, and pulling assertively (but don't jerk!) on the reins to get him to stop, *now*. Don't use more rein pressure than is needed, but use enough to get the job done promptly. Release pressure for a moment when he does stop to reward his response. Then back him up a few steps, stop, and stand for a moment so he can think about it.

Lets his shoulder run ahead of his rear end in the Two-Tracking: Slow the shoulder down by applying pres-sure on the rein that's on the side he's moving toward (direct rein). For example, if you're Two-Tracking to the left, apply pressure on the left rein by bringing it back toward your belly button to lay it against his neck, and "catch" his rear end up by using your leg more aggres-sively behind neutral position.

"Dives" into the new direction after the change: If he drops his shoulder and tries to change course after the lead change (for example, tries to go to the right after changing to the right lead), you've lost control of his shoulders and need to get it back. To do so, use the Backing-in-a-Circle exercise I describe on p. 123.

# 10 GETTING READY TO SHOW

You've worked hard with your horse to bring him this far; now it's time to get him—and you—ready to compete. If you're going to be showing in National Reining Horse Association (NRHA)-sanctioned events, you'll have to ride your horse one-handed in a bridle. So, I'll talk first about moving your horse from a snaffle into a transition bit and then to a bridle bit (see also my earlier discussion of bits on p. 26).

Later, I'll fine-tune some of the maneuvers you've already learned, to get them "competition-ready." I'll also explain how to get the most out of your practice sessions at home.

Now is also a good time to get very familiar with the rule book of the association in which you'll be showing. In particular, learn the general rules, what constitutes illegal equipment, and so on. For example, did you know it's a five-point penalty in NRHA competition to hold onto the saddle with either one or both hands? Learn what else will cost you precious points.

## Putting Your Horse in the Bridle

You've been working your horse in a ring snaffle up to this point. If you are planning to show in local reining or breed-sanctioned events, such as with the American Quarter Horse Association (AQHA) or American Paint Horse Association (APHA), your horse can stay in a snaffle or hackamore for junior-division competition up through his five-year-old year. If your horse is three or older and you plan to compete in NRHA events, however, he needs to be in a "bridle." (As I mentioned in chapter 3, a headstall and shank bit is commonly called a "bridle," while a headstall and snaffle bit is simply a "snaffle.")

That said, my advice is to stay in a ring snaffle as long as you can. Everything you've worked on up to now is core training, meant to be perfected in a snaffle whether your horse is two or ten. The goal is for your horse to be "soft" everywhere in his body, and to stay soft through all maneuvers and transitions. Only then, when you are both truly proficient in all the exercises, should you consider transitioning into the bridle.

Riders often turn to a bridle for the wrong reasons.

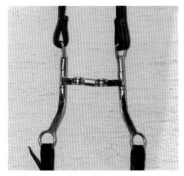

**10.1** Shank snaffle
This is a good transition bit between a plain ring snaffle and a bridle bit. It acts a little like a snaffle and also a little like a shank bit, giving a horse time to adjust to the difference in signal between a snaffle and a regular bit. (Note: this bit is ordinarily used with a curb strap.)

**10.2** Short-shank correction bit
This transition bit is jointed in two places around its port, which is fairly low and wide, and can act severely on the bars of the mouth if the reins are jerked. In quiet, educated hands, this bit encourages flexion and collection, plus gives you good lateral control.

**10.3** Long-shank correction bit
This bit potentially delivers a lot of force on the bars of the mouth. In skilled hands, however, it can promote considerable flexion and precision on a horse that needs a little bit more leverage than shorter shanks can provide.

You move your horse from a ring snaffle into a transition bit, and from there into a regular bridle bit. Both transition and bridle bits feature *shank* cheek pieces. The length of the shank determines the degree of leverage (pressure) on the horse's bars, chin, and poll (by way of the chin strap). Shorter shanks generally have a milder effect, while longer shanks exert more pressure and thus should be reserved for trained horses that are responsive to subtle cues.

In addition, these bits generally have a *port*, which is a curved section in the mouthpiece. The port exerts pressure on the horse's tongue and the roof of his mouth. The amount of pressure is determined by the height and width of the curve—lower, wider ports are considered less severe than higher, narrower ones.

Consider these characteristics when choosing a transition or bridle bit for your horse.

### Transition Bits

A good transition bit helps to confirm what your horse has already learned in a ring snaffle, without the confusing signals that can occur when you just put him straight into a solid-mouthed shank bit. A transition bit feels a little like a snaffle, and a little like a shank bit, thus "splits the difference" between the two to give your horse time to adjust (figs. 10.1, 10.2, and 10.3).

I usually start the transition process with a shank snaffle* or short-shank correction bit. Although they have shanks and a curb strap (thus exert leverage on the bars of the horse's mouth and chin groove), these bits are less confusing to the horse than a solid-mouthed bit due to their flexibility and the fact that you can still pull laterally if you need to. They can be "loose-jawed" or "loose-shanked," meaning the shank cheek pieces are jointed and move easily, giving your horse a little lead time between when you pick up the rein and when the "message" reaches his mouth. And that, in turn, aids him in staying relaxed as he learns to interpret the pressure he's feeling in new places (as compared to how it felt in a ring snaffle). The extra "jointedness" of these bits also allows a greater separation of signals going from one side of

**10.4** Loose-jawed shank bit

**This Gordon Hayes loose-jawed bit is a favorite of mine for competition. Sensitive horses like it, as it has a lot of "feel" (it easily transmits the subtlest of cues) in the jointed shanks. And, although it's powerful enough to control a horse whose adrenaline gets flowing, in the right hands, it doesn't cause resistance or mouth-gapping. If necessary, I put latex tape on the chain to soften it.**

**10.5** Spanish bit

**This type of bit derives from the vaqueros and is still popular in California, but you'll see them more often on cow horses than on reiners. This one features a lot of silver ornament.**

### Regular Bridle Bits

Most of these have a solid (not jointed) mouthpiece and longer shanks, and come in many variations.

Thicker mouthpieces distribute the pressure over wider areas of the tongue and bars, which makes them less severe than thinner mouthpieces.

As mentioned earlier, higher ports are generally more severe than lower ones, although the thickness of the mouthpiece and the width of the tongue relief in the port (that is, the space of the port that allows the tongue to come up into it) also factor into how severe the bit actually feels to the horse.

The shanks or cheek pieces may be solid or "loose-jawed," meaning jointed. Solid cheek pieces transmit cues with less "slack," thus may be good for duller and stronger horses. Loose-jawed cheek pieces suit sensitive or "feely" horses best, as there's more transfer time between the start of a rein signal and engagement of the bit. The high-port, loose-jawed bit made by Gordon Hayes is one of my favorites (fig. 10.4).

the mouth to the other, which enhances the clarity of your cues from side to side, and makes your signals less confusing for your horse.

Because of the manner in which the correction bit is jointed in two places around its port, it can potentially act severely on the bars of the mouth when the reins are jerked. In quiet hands, however, the short-shank correction bit is great for encouraging flexion and collection, plus it gives you good lateral control.

You can soften these bits even further by using a thick leather curb strap (instead of a chain), or wrapping latex bandage tape around the chain or the mouthpiece to protect the bars of your horse's mouth.

When your horse is completely comfortable and responding well to neck-reining in a transition bit, you can move him up to a regular bridle bit.

I should also mention the Spanish bridle bits, which derive from the vaqueros and are still popular in California, where they're more often seen on cow horses than on reiners (fig. 10.5).

*Note: Strictly speaking (especially from a classical standpoint), any bit with shanks and a curb strap (and thus leverage on the bars of the mouth) is not a true "snaffle." Still, the term "shank snaffle" to describe a bit with a broken mouthpiece has become standard usage among Western riders and trainers, so I'm using it here.

Specifically, a "bigger bridle" (meaning a stronger, leveraged shank bit) isn't the answer if your problem is lack of control. For that, you need to go back to basics and establish that you, not your horse, is the one who calls the shots on speed and direction. (Review chapter 6 on collection and steering, if need be.) With the exception of safety (as when your horse absolutely won't stop even with a basics "tune-up"), the only valid reason for graduating to a bridle is to achieve a higher level of precision and collection, and only when both you and your horse are ready for it.

Bits, like all equipment, can be used to intimidate or to educate. The severity of a bit, ultimately, is literally in the hands of the rider. As you begin to transition into a bridle, you must be extra soft with your hands and extra patient to avoid scaring your horse and making him "shocky" or overreactive in the face. For horses (and for humans, if you think about it), a tense mouth naturally results in a tense body.

### Beginning the Transition

When you and your horse are ready to work for greater precision and one-handed control, start by selecting a transition bit your horse seems comfortable with—usually a short-shank correction bit or a shank snaffle (see sidebar, pp. 127–8). Try several good bits, keeping in mind that what suits your horse best may change frequently. (And you may ultimately find that one bit works fine at home, while you need a slightly stronger one when you show.)

When your horse is comfortably bitted in a transition bit, continue to carry the reins in two hands, but move your hands closer together (fig. 10.6). Back when you started work on the various exercises in this book, with your horse in a snaffle, your hands were naturally fairly wide apart, especially if your horse is a youngster. Over time, your hands should have begun to move closer together and act more as one.

Now, with your horse in the transition bit, it's time

**10.6** Hand position

**Once your horse is comfortably bitted in a transition bit, continue at first to carry the reins in two hands, but bring your hands closer together and be sure to move them slowly while your horse adjusts to the new bit.**

to begin keeping your hands as close together as possible. Focus on laying the indirect rein (what will become the *neck-rein*) against your horse's neck to signal a turn, while using the direct rein only to make sure his nose always leads the turn. The combination of indirect and direct rein cues will gradually teach the horse to respond to the neck-rein alone, which will allow you to eventually ride one-handed.

It's more important now than ever to move your hands slowly, even half-speed. Take the slack out of the reins gradually to give your horse time to think and respond, and use the minimum amount of rein pressure possible to get the job done.

The new pressure points your horse will be feeling via his new bit can be confusing for him, so go easy. I think of it as always giving my horse a place to go and plenty of time to get there!

With that in mind, now's a good time to do a lot of trail riding. This gives your horse a chance to get used to the feel of the bit and the slightly different position of your hands, while the natural obstacles of the trail help him understand what he's supposed to do. Neck-rein around trees and bushes, and use open areas to lope circles. Relax and enjoy the ride; don't hurry.

After your horse acclimates to his new bit, resume working on all the exercises you've learned to this point. Keep your cues the same, but, again, wait for your horse to understand and respond to the different feel.

### Going to One Hand

When your horse is responding well to neck-rein pressure and seems completely comfortable in his new bit, begin carrying the reins in your left hand only. Split reins are ordinarily held with the index finger between them, and the rein "tails" on the left side of the horse's neck and withers (see fig. 10.8 A). During the transition period, however, cross the reins over themselves to allow your whole hand to be between them, with one rein on each side of his neck. This enables you to keep tipping your horse's nose in the direction of movement a while longer as he gets more and more used to moving off the neck-rein (figs. 10.7 A & B).

Continue to review all exercises. Riding one-handed, you may feel as if you're starting all over again! If so, just go slow and give your horse time to adjust. When your steering and collection on all previous exercises feels pretty flawless at all speeds, progress to holding your reins in your left hand with just your index finger between them (figs. 10.8 A–C). This is when I like to work on any steering exercises I can

dream up, at every possible variation of speed and size of circle. I reach down with my free hand to tug the direct rein any time my horse doesn't go nose first into a turn, and I put both hands on the reins to overcorrect any guiding problems (figs. 10.9 A & B).

Keep working your horse in the transition bit until you feel reasonably certain that he:

► thoroughly understands the new pressure on his mouth

► holds the bit in a comfortable manner

► stays relaxed when you're riding him in it

► guides well with one hand at all speeds

► can perform all of the exercises you taught him in a snaffle

**10.7 A & B** Crossing the reins

When your horse is responding well to being ridden with two hands in his transition bit, begin carrying the reins in your left hand only. Cross one rein over the other, like this, to enable you to continue tipping your horse's nose in the direction of movement for a while (A). Notice how this crossed-over hold makes it relatively easy for me to tip my horse's head to the inside as I lope a circle (B).

B

**10.8 A–C** Proper rein grip

Ultimately, you should hold your split reins as shown with only your index finger between the two reins (A). If you use romal or "California style" reins, they come up through the bottom of your left hand, which should hold them firmly. The romal is held by your right hand (B). With these rein holds, you have less ability to directly affect how your horse bends through the neck (C). (By now, of course, he should be starting to do it right on his own!)

**10.9 A & B** Turning
Here's how to get a bit of extra help in turning right with the standard split-rein hold (A), and turning left (B).

When all that's in place, it's time to move into a regular bridle bit. Even then, when your horse is quite secure in his neck-reining, remember you always have the option of returning to two hands as necessary to tip his nose, or lift his shoulder, or help him overcome confusion in any maneuver.

Be patient! The Spanish vaqueros thought nothing of taking two years to put a horse into the bridle. So take the time it takes.

## Fine-Tuning

Regardless of whether you'll be showing one-handed or two, there are a few parts of your horse's education that need fine-tuning before you ride him into that show pen. These include speeding up the spin and "shutting it off" (stopping precisely), as well as helping him to clearly understand the different cues for a spin, a rollback, and a backup.

I'll talk about each of these in turn.

### Speeding Up the Spin

Even when your goal is to build speed into your spin, *always* start this maneuver slowly, to decrease anticipa-

---

---

tion and increase correctness. Whenever you're working at home, preferably go one entire revolution slowly, or at least until your horse hits his "sweet spot," meaning the place where he relaxes and is moving around comfortably, with cadence.

Then begin to build speed by "clucking" in rhythm with your horse's footfalls, gradually speeding your "clucking" to speed up his feet.

## It Ain't So

**MYTH: If my horse seems too strong in my hands, I need a stronger bit.**

This may be one of the most damaging fallacies out there. A horse's mouth needs to be educated, so you should never put more bit in his mouth than he has the training to be comfortable with. Only as he gets lighter and more responsive, can you use "more" bit, to enable your cues to become ever more subtle.

Putting a "bigger" bit on a horse just because you can't control him in the one you're using is generally counter-productive. It's better to go back to basics in a snaffle, and address the control problem that way. Unless your horse absolutely refuses to slow down for you (even after a review of the "basics"), "bigger" bits should be reserved for fine-tuning.

If your horse doesn't speed up in response to your leg pressure at the cinch and your vocal cue, *do not* try to correct him by kicking or spurring him vigorously. As I discussed in chapter 8, if he gets punished (for any reason) while in the spin, he'll come to dread spinning, and, believe me, you don't want that!

In reality, if he resists speeding up, it's probably because he wasn't properly between your hands and your feet in the first place—in other words, he wasn't moving off your outside (indirect) rein and leg. So if you just kick to insist on speed, in addition to punishing him in the spin, you'll simply be driving him "faster, wronger."

Instead, stop and fix what's not working by side-passing or counter-arcing off your outside (indirect) rein and leg. (For example, if he was resisting in a spin to the right, sidepass or counter-arc him to the right, as you learned to do toward the end of chapter 7, p. 94.)

At this point, go ahead and use your leg and spur as aggressively as necessary at or just behind the cinch to insist that he get moving laterally, quickly. Then, go right into a spin (the opposite way from the direction he was spinning originally, as he'll now be bent that way from the counter-arc) and *let* him turn, as opposed to forcing him. This way, he thinks of the spin as the good place to be (compared to the correction of the sidepass or counter-arc), and doesn't come to resist it.

Continue spinning in the opposite direction for a bit, and you'll likely have reason to correct him again with a sidepass or counter-arc, which will then set you up to again spin in the original direction.

Through all this, your horse must move his shoulders when you move your reins. In other words, when your hands move to the side to start the turn, your horse's shoulders should stay between the reins, which means his feet should start moving laterally. If he knows better but doesn't respond, let his outside elbow "bump into" your outside foot to remind him.

If he starts to stiffen up throughout his body, stop spinning and drive him forward into your hands until he softens in the face, then start again.

### "Shutting Off" the Spin

To avoid penalties, your horse must stop precisely where

the pattern dictates. In other words, when the pattern calls for four revolutions, it means four, period—you can't over- or under-spin more than a shoulder-width (or one-eighth of the circumference of the circle) without penalty. Believe me, that's not much margin for error!

To fine-tune the spin's stop, say "Whoa" and use a bit of outside rein to help your horse's shoulders cease movement. If he keeps going anyway, move him immediately into a spin in the opposite direction for a revolution or two, before saying "Whoa" again. If he fails to stop precisely again, go back to spinning in the original direction and continue back and forth like this until he'll stop completely at "Whoa." Then sit and let him relax a moment or two as a reward.

Remember, you don't want him to equate spinning with being punished, so make it routine and workmanlike in each direction, as you strive for precision in the spin's stop.

The ultimate goal is for him to stop the spin cold when you say "Whoa" *and* drop your hand (as opposed to "helping" stop his outside shoulder), so work on that next, using the same strategy.

As I stressed in chapter 8, always remember to count your spins. No matter how badly a spin starts, as you come around to your starting place, say "That's one," then the next time, "That's two," and so on. If you routinely do this at home while practicing, you'll never forget to count when you're at a show—something that's otherwise awfully easy to do, given the excitement and stress of competing.

### Differentiating Cues

Before you compete, you must have your cues for the spin, the rollback, and the backup clearly differentiated in your horse's mind. For this to occur, you must ask for each of these a bit differently, and be absolutely consistent about those differences each time you ask.

Here's how to differentiate for each maneuver:

Spin—always *step forward* into your spins. Close both your legs in neutral position and drive your horse forward one step before initiating the cues for the spin.

Rollback—after riding all the way to the "bottom" of your stop, look in the direction you want to go and slowly and smoothly draw your rein hand toward that turn-side belt loop. Once your horse is committed to the turn (but not before), begin to reinforce the rollback with your outside leg at the cinch, and "cluck."

Backup—always *hesitate* for a heartbeat at the end of the stop. Then softly draw both reins straight back toward your belly button, and hold your horse equally with both your legs, so he doesn't turn. Once he begins backing-up, make sure he's going straight before you ask him to increase his speed.

## At-Home Practice before the Show

A common complaint, especially among rookie reiners, is: "How come my horse doesn't perform at a show the way he schools at home?" Theoretically, he knows all the maneuvers and he knows how to respond to your corrections when he errs; so why the disheartening difference?

The answer is obvious when you think about it: you don't ride him at home the way you do at the show—in a multitude of small but significant ways.

The sensible solution, then, is to begin schooling him at home as if you're already at the show, well before the time you actually head out to compete. "Cut him loose," so to speak, and stop protecting him from making mistakes.

How do you do this? When you feel as if you're ready to start showing, begin working the following strategies into your daily practice:

Use only one hand more often. If you'll be showing one-handed, ride one-handed as much as you can. Try to avoid reaching down to pull a rein with the other hand, or "slipping" a rein (making one rein shorter than the other).

Also, pay attention to your horse's neck-reining—can you guide him one-handed when he's out of frame, and keep him on track as you gather him up again?

Check your "cluck" or "kiss." Is your horse automatically "dialed in" to an increase in speed when he hears you "cluck" or "kiss"? In the show pen, you want that response to be automatic, so you don't have to reinforce it.

Cool it on corrections. Don't correct your horse as quickly as you have been doing; see if you can smooth over any rough patches, minimizing the mistake without making any obvious correction.

"Test" your maneuvers. Ride all the maneuvers as if you're in the show pen to see how they "work." It's been my experience that when I walk through the gate at a show, I have half the good stuff I had at home, and twice the bad! So be sure your horse is really as right as he can be. Specifically check:

▶ *Lead departures*—In a class, you're not going to be able to give your horse the cue ten times before get-

ting him to lope off. Can you get it right the first time?

▶ *Circles*—Is your horse going to speed up out of control if you give him the reins? Or lose the shape of the circle or the frame of his body? Better find out now!

▶ *Lead changes*—You won't be able to wait to change leads until everything is perfect, the way you like to at home. Can your horse "get his change" on a large, fast circle when you ask for it in the center of the pen?

▶ *Rundowns and stops*—Will he run a straight line with minimal guidance, on a loose rein and without increasing speed unless asked to? Try it a lot! Can you keep your hand down when you stop him?

▶ *Spins*—Can you get some cadence going and add some speed before two revolutions? If not, you won't be able to get up to speed in just four revolutions at a show. Can you stop spinning on the mark, with your hand down, just by saying "Whoa"? After the spin, can you continue right on with a loose rein? You won't be able to sit for a while until your horse calms down, the way you like to at home.

▶ *Rollbacks*—Can you hurry him out of the rollback, the way you need to at a show, without his getting "on the muscle" or leaning? You can't practice this a lot, of course, as it'll lead to anticipation. But you'd better check now and then to be sure that you *can* do it.

# 11  AT THE SHOW

The day has arrived. It's time to wow the world (or at least the crowd in the stands) with what you and your horse can do. In this chapter, I discuss strategies for show day, including your mental outlook, your performance goals, and your "body English" in the show pen.

I also talk you through an actual pattern, and explain how the scoring works.

Finally, we'll do some troubleshooting together so you can prepare to deal with (or head off) the things that most often go wrong in the show pen.

## Show-Day Strategies

When it's time to compete, the mental part of the game becomes critically important. We all get "butterflies"; the challenge is to get them all loping in the same direction! You do this by disciplining yourself to derive satisfaction from a job well done rather than by how you place. Personally, I'd rather be fourth after doing well against tough competition, than first after a less-than-my-best performance that's the "least bad" that day.

Remember, too, that how a class is placed comes down to *one* person's opinion on *one* given day. By focusing simply on turning in the best performance you can on that day, given your horse's level of training, *you* become the ultimate judge. No matter how you place, you're giving yourself credit for reaching your own goals, plus getting a valuable learning experience out of it.

To accomplish all this, it helps to be a bit "Zen." Being in a zone of readiness, yet calm and relaxed, enables you to maintain the right perspective while performing at your peak. You've already prepared yourself for this state of "calm confidence" by doing your homework diligently before the show (see chapter 10); later in this chapter I'll talk about being prepared for all eventualities—knowing you're ready for anything also helps you stay calm.

In your first few shows, don't worry about trying to get above a score of zero on any of your maneuvers; just try to stay out of the penalty box. At a lot of smaller shows, you can actually win classes with this strategy (which results in an overall score of 70—more on that when I talk about scoring—see p. 146).

Once you've acquired a bit of show experience, move up to trying to "plus" the maneuvers your horse is capable of "plussing," but still be content to "zero" the others. In other words, don't expect somehow to pull something off that hasn't been happening at home. That's one human habit that horses find particularly annoying!

This goes double for speed. Don't ask for more speed than your horse can give and still stay relaxed and cadenced. It's always more pleasing to see a horse go a tiny bit slower and *look* as if he could go faster, than to see his rider push him and learn for certain that he falls apart at the higher speed.

If you follow these general guidelines, you and your horse will develop enough confidence in each other to put together good runs that will just get better over time.

### A Word about Turnout

You're being judged from the moment you enter the arena, and first impressions do count. It's not that the judge will deduct a half point because your horse's bridle path is a 2-inch Mohawk. Still, it's only human nature that a pleasing presentation prompts the observer to look for good things to come. If you appear sloppy and unprofessional, the judge will subconsciously expect to see a weak performance. And it's much harder to win him or her back to the positive side if that first impression is negative. Take pride in your and your horse's appearance.

### Proper "Body English" in the Show Pen

When you ride into the arena, jitters can make your own body feel foreign to you. This, in turn, makes it harder to ride the way you know you should—and the way you have been at home.

Here are some tips for each part of your body to keep your horsemanship "up and running."

Your eyes: Look ahead, not down at your horse. On circles, look one-quarter of the circle ahead; it will help your horse know where he's supposed to go.

As you approach the center for a lead change, look straight ahead, not in the new direction you'll be taking. This helps keep your horse from anticipating the change or plunging prematurely into the new direction.

On spins, look slightly in the direction you're going. If you look in the opposite direction (don't laugh—lots of people do this!), you can cause your shoulder and therefore your horse's shoulder to drop, creating "drag." If you tend to get dizzy, look right between your horse's ears, at his poll.

On the rundown, look up and far ahead, not down at the spot where you hope to stop, which "short-stops" your horse's action.

On the rollback, look in the direction you're going to go (and "follow" your gaze with your hand).

Your torso: Sit up straight, neither leaning forward (especially on your lead departures and stops) nor falling behind your horse's motion (especially in rundowns). Don't "pump" with your pelvis or torso.

Your shoulders: Keep them back and squared to your horse's shoulders. This is essential to keeping your horse's shoulders up and even, and not leaning. (In other words, if you drop your shoulder, your horse will drop his.)

Your rein hand: Keep it quiet and soft, within an imaginary 6-inch box right around the area of the saddle horn. (Remember, in the beginning, this was a much bigger box, and you're working to shrink it as your horse becomes more and more responsive—see p. 129.)

Be careful not to let your rein hand drag down to the left, or move around with your horse's motion. Also avoid using it to encourage your horse to go faster.

As you neck-rein to the right, don't let your hand

go too far right, which shortens the left rein and forces your horse to look left—the opposite of what you want. Make sure your hand moves toward your turn-side belt loop.

As you neck-rein to the left, don't pull back too much and cause your horse to back up instead of turn.

Your right arm: Keep it tucked in at waist level (figs. 11.1 A & B). If you allow it to be "free," it can take on a life of its own, doing such things as flopping and pumping in the rundown—very distracting! It also can result in a "drag" in your left spins, or cause you to lean in on your right spins.

Your legs: These should stay quietly at your horse's sides, where you can use them quickly at need. No gripping—that just signals your horse to go faster. Your heels should be down, with the ball of your foot on the stirrup. Your legs should never get "behind" you, as this just tips you forward and out of balance.

Don't let your legs stick out. Be especially careful when spinning to the right that your right foot doesn't sneak forward (or the left sneak forward in a left spin). A too-forward foot can cause your horse not to want to turn quickly in that direction. It also causes your hips to twist in the opposite direction, which gives your horse mixed signals ("turn—no, don't turn").

## Riding a Pattern

Now let's go maneuver-by-maneuver through an actual reining pattern. We'll use the NRHA Pattern 6, as it's a basic one that's common at weekend shows (fig. 11.2). The pattern you actually ride in your class may be different, but there will be enough common elements to make this "talk-through" valuable to you. (Note: you can find all the current NRHA reining patterns at www.nrha.com.)

For learning purposes, it helps to have a knowledgeable critique of your run, so ask your trainer (or any trainer at the gate when it's time for your go) to watch you ride and provide feedback. If possible, also have a friend record your run on video so you can analyze it later at your leisure—again, ideally with your trainer or a knowledgeable friend.

### Your Entrance

As you walk to the center of the arena, look confident and relaxed—even if you're scared to death. Take a few deep "belly breaths" (drawing the air down into your abdomen) along the way. This will aid your relaxation and your horse's; remember, he's as nervous as you are to be out in that arena all by himself.

Resist the temptation to constantly bump the bridle reins. It's almost like a nervous "tic," and it just makes it appear you're having trouble getting your horse to soften to the bridle.

When you get to the center of the arena (and make sure it really is the center—nerves often make competitors misjudge this) stop and hesitate long enough to take a deep breath. (In fact, whenever you see the word "hesitate" in a pattern, plan to stop long enough to take a breath. This ensures not only that you hesitate enough for the judge to see it, but also that you breathe at least three or four times during your run!)

### Four Spins Right

After your hesitation, as you lift your rein hand to prepare for the first spin to the right, consciously *slow your hand down*. Specifically, as the left rein moves against your horse's neck, pause a fraction of a second to allow him to acknowledge the cue. Otherwise, adrenaline can cause you to move your hand more rapidly than your horse is accustomed to feeling. And then, when you don't feel him preparing to turn (because he's still figuring out what you want), you pull harder and even faster to the right. That tips his head to the left, the opposite of what you want, and so keeps him from getting started properly into the spin. So, think "slow"

A

**11.1 A & B** Correct vs. incorrect arm position

Many riders don't know what to do with their right arm, especially in the show pen. *Correct:* For best results and a polished look, keep it tucked in a natural position at waist level (A).

*Incorrect:* Here's what *not* to do with your right arm—allow it to hang down or be "free" (B). If you do, it can wind up flopping or pumping in the rundown—very distracting.

B

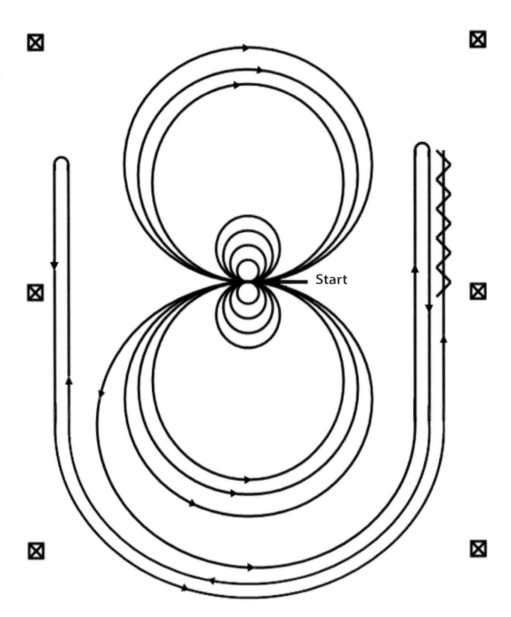

Start

**11.2** National Reining Horse Association (NRHA) Pattern 6

Walk or trot to the center of the arena. Begin there, facing the left wall or fence:

1 Four spins to right. Hesitate.

2 Four spins to left. Hesitate.

3 Pick up left lead, three circles to left—the first two large and fast, the third small and slow. Lead change at center of arena.

4 Three circles to right—the first two large and fast, the third small and slow. Lead change at center of arena.

5 Begin large, fast circle to left, but don't close this circle. Run up right side of arena, past center marker; do right rollback at least 20 feet from wall or fence—no hesitation.

6 Continue back around previous circle, but don't close this circle. Run up left side of arena, past center marker, and do left rollback at least 20 feet from wall or fence—no hesitation.

7 Continue back around previous circle, but don't close this circle. Run up right side of arena, past center marker, and do sliding stop at least 20 feet from wall or fence. Back up at least 10 feet. Hesitate to demonstrate completion of pattern.

and you'll more likely move your hand at your usual speed.

As you start to spin, remember to count! Spins that start less than smoothly are the most difficult to remember to count, but they are also the ones where it's most important as it's easy to get confused. By now, if you've been faithfully counting every time you spin at home, it should be almost automatic for you.

At the completion of four spins, remember to raise your hand slightly to block any further motion as you say "Whoa," so your horse stops precisely where he should.

Then hesitate and breathe.

### Four Spins Left

If you don't stop right on the mark after your right-hand spins, don't try to realign your horse before beginning your left-hand spins. You're not going to fool the judge; he's right in front of you. Plus, if your horse misinterprets and starts his left spin, it looks rough. That's why it's best, regardless of where you've stopped, just to pick up your hand slowly to the left and start your four spins.

Be mindful of your hand, because when you spin to the left, it's especially easy to pull back too much, which will cause your horse to rock back and "get tangled" in his spin.

If you need to "cluck" to keep your horse's feet moving, try to do it in the spot where you'd otherwise be counting, as it's hard to "cluck" and count separately. Make the "cluck" your count.

Again, strive to "shut off" your last spin in the correct spot. It's a bummer to earn a half-point with a good spin, only to be penalized a half-point for going a step too far.

Then hesitate and breathe.

### Three Circles Left

It's okay to walk several steps (but *do not* trot!) as you prepare to pick up your left lead. So take the time you need to set your horse up correctly to step off into the correct lead. Specifically, as you walk those steps, push your horse's hip to the left and tip his nose to the left. When he feels soft in your hand and his body is correct, use your right leg behind neutral position and "kiss." Be sure to lope the first couple of strides straight.

Your first two circles to the left are the large, fast ones. Allow your horse to build smoothly to his ideal speed over the first quarter of the first circle. By that time, you'll be profiled to the judge, so try by then to be going the speed you intend to maintain. As I discussed earlier, ask for only as much speed as your horse can manage without losing his steering or brakes.

Incline your upper body forward a bit (it reinforces the impression of "moving right along"), but keep your bottom in the saddle, driving your horse forward. Move your rein hand just slightly forward.

Keep looking to the left as you begin your second large, fast circle, so your body language doesn't make your horse think about changing leads. Don't slack off on your speed; keep your second large circle the same size and speed as the first.

As you approach the center of the arena at the end of your second large circle, take a deep breath and exhale (try humming—I find it helps) as you melt into the saddle and draw your horse back to a slower lope. At the same time, squeeze him up with both your legs—your outside leg especially—so he doesn't break gait or fall out of lead. Allow him a stride or two on each side of center to reduce his speed, then guide him into the smaller circle. Use the rest of your small, slow circle to relax and *breathe*.

### Lead Change

Three-fourths of the way through your small circle, begin to prepare to change leads. Apply a little pressure on your right rein to straighten your horse's neck, and a little pressure in neutral position with your right leg to straighten his body. This will also prevent him from changing before you ask him to.

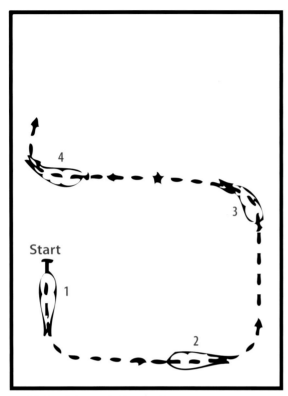

**11.3 A** Lead change (wide arena)

**If the show arena is large enough, ride your lead change (star) like this, as a straight line across the center of the pen.**

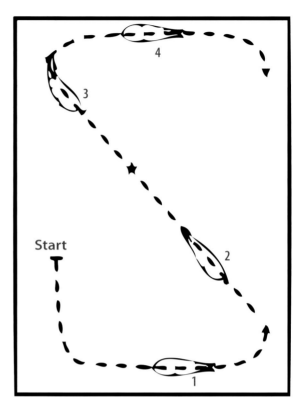

**11.3 B** Lead change (narrow arena)

**If the show arena is narrow across the middle, make your change (star) along a diagonal line through the center; this will give you a bit more room so you can keep straight for the change.**

Technically, you have a stride on each side of the arena's dead center to change leads without penalty, so you need to be as precise as possible (fig. 11.3 A). Right at the center, take your right leg off, apply pressure with your left behind neutral position, and "kiss." Keep your horse's body straight, and continue straight for a couple of strides after the change (remember—never let a change of leads become an automatic change of direction). Don't slow down, either; just roll right along.

If the arena is narrow across the middle, make your change along a diagonal line, instead. This will give you a bit more room so you can keep your horse straight (fig. 11.3 B).

### Three Circles Right

Going to the right you'll again have two large, fast circles first. Make them the same size and speed as the left large circles, building smoothly to your horse's ideal speed just as you did going to the left. The tracks of your large right and large left circles should just touch in the center of the arena.

As you come across the center toward the judge at the end of your second large circle, begin to transition to the small, slow circle by again taking a deep breath and exhaling, melting into the saddle, and "drawing your horse to you." Remember to "squeeze him up" with both your legs so he doesn't break gait or fall out of lead.

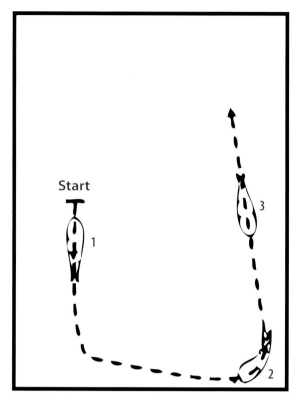

**11.4** Using the corner

If you are riding a pattern in a narrow arena, or if your horse tends to lean toward the rail along the long sides, go a bit deeper into the corner before you start your rundown (2), and then slightly angle your line in toward the center of the pen (3).

Reduce speed a stride or two on each side of the center, then use the small, slow circle to relax and *breathe*.

### Lead Change

As you approach the three-quarter point of the small circle, start to apply slight left rein and leg pressure in neutral position to straighten your horse's body, and at the center point, remove your left leg and apply pressure with your right behind neutral, and "kiss." Again, keep holding your horse straight through his body and in his line of travel.

### Rundown, Stop

Now increase your speed as you round the top of the arena on the left lead. I like to square the corner at the top so my horse is straight from the first stride of the rundown. If the arena is narrow or if your horse tends to lean toward the rail, you can go a bit deeper into the corner and then angle your line in toward the center a bit (fig. 11.4).

Be sure to look up and gradually build speed for a long, straight run "into the next ZIP code." Don't let your horse jump into his rundown as if he's being shot from a cannon. Ride with authority, accelerating smoothly until the point where you say "Whoa." Be sure to stay at least 20 feet from the arena fence in the rundown, and go way past the center marker before you stop. If you run long, your horse will stay truer in his rundowns. If you go short, it won't result in the best performance, plus your horse will start scotching ("stutter-stopping," or anticipating the stop) in future rundowns.

Remember not to pull when you do say "Whoa"; wait a moment and then pull only if you must.

### Rollback Right

Get all the way to the "bottom" of your stop before cueing for the rollback, but once your horse *has* stopped, don't hesitate before beginning the rollback—still at least 20 feet from the fence. Again, slow your hand down and make sure not to come across your horse's neck, which would cause his head to go left. Instead, draw your left hand back at an angle toward your right side belt loop as you look right. Let him get the rollback started slowly, nose-first to the right, then once he's committed to it, "kiss" and use your outside leg at the cinch. After the 180-degree turn, move right back into a lope. There's no penalty for coming out of the rollback on the wrong lead, but you must be on the correct lead (right) before you go into the corner. If you need to change, it's easiest to do it just as you're going into the corner.

### Rundown, Stop

As you go around the end of the arena, set your run up just as you did the first time, either squaring your corner or going deep and angling toward the middle of the pen a bit at least 20 feet off the fence.

Again, build the speed of your run smoothly, go well past the center marker, and ride right up to the "Whoa," waiting to pull on the reins—and doing so only if you have to.

### Rollback Left

Be sure to come to a full stop, but don't hesitate before looking left and slowly moving your hand for the left rollback. Don't pull back too much; remember, that will get him "tangled up." Draw him slowly left (moving your hand toward your left side belt loop) and once he's committed, "kiss" and use your right leg at the cinch.

Again, change to the correct lead (left) if necessary just before going into the corner.

### Rundown, Stop

Square the corner once again, and if all has gone well, you might run a little faster to your last stop. Again, be sure to pass your middle marker before stopping, but don't go as far as the first two rundowns. Stay at least 20 feet from the fence.

At the "bottom" of that stop, pause briefly before beginning the backup to be sure your horse isn't thinking about rolling back.

### Back Up

Pull straight back, softly, holding him with both legs, and start backing him up. Once your horse is backing-up straight, "cluck" and bump with both legs for speed and cadence.

After backing-up straight for at least 10 feet, stop and hesitate to show completion of the pattern.

### Your Exit

You're done! Mentally pat yourself on the back (and actually pat your horse on the neck or hip) as you walk out of the arena. Don't forget to look at the judge's card and watch your video so you can improve for next time.

And, speaking of that judge's card, let's talk in greater detail about scoring.

## Scoring the Maneuvers

The ideal a judge has in mind when evaluating a class of reiners comes from the "A. General" section of the NRHA rule book. It says, in part: "To rein a horse is not only to guide him, but also to control his every movement. The best reined horse should be willingly guided or controlled with little or no apparent resistance and dictated to completely."

With that ideal in mind, the judge scores each reining pattern on a scale from 0 to infinity, with most runs scoring in the 60 to 80 range. A score of 70 denotes an "average" performance (see below). It may be a decent run, nothing barn-burning but all the maneuvers performed correctly with no penalties. Or it may be a blistering run with a bunch of penalties. (That's why, as we discussed earlier in this chapter, your first job is to stay out of the penalty box—you can't afford to give points away.)

Each pattern typically comprises seven or eight maneuvers. Usually, a set of three circles with lead change is counted as one maneuver. The approach to the stop, the stop itself, and the rollback (or backup) are another. Right spins are one; left spins are one. The ten NRHA patterns are varied combinations of these basic maneuvers.

The judge evaluates and scores each maneuver individually; a scribe then writes that maneuver's score and any penalty points down on the score card. The scores for each maneuver are added (or, if they're negative, subtracted) from the "average" overall score of 70, and then any penalty points are subtracted to create the final, total score for the run. The score of 70 is what a team would receive if they ran the pattern with no mistakes, but without exhibition of superior ability or any particular flair. One judge I know explains that 70 is "room temperature," and the scores "heat up" (get better) or "cool down" (get worse) from there.

In scoring, the judge must ascertain that you are "on pattern" (i.e., you're executing the called-for maneuvers in the proper order), and that you perform each maneuver correctly. Smoothness, finesse, attitude, quickness, authority, and controlled speed all contribute to the impression you make.

The judge also considers the "degree of difficulty" for each maneuver, and this is typically related to speed and quickness. For example, a perfectly executed *fast* spin will score higher than an equally perfectly executed *slow* one.

For each maneuver, the point scoring is as follows:

► -1 ½ for an extremely poor execution
► -1 for very poor
► - ½ for poor
► 0 for correct
► +½ for good execution
► +1 for very good
► + 1 ½ for excellent

Penalty points, of course, can negate the effect of a plus score on any maneuver. For example, a "+½" spin can incur a "-½" penalty for over- or underspinning an eighth of a circle, thus negating the credit. (For a complete listing of penalty points, refer to your NRHA rule book—which comes to you annually with NRHA membership.)

### Getting a "Feel" for It

Scoring is fairly subjective, and sometimes the difference between 0 and +½ is hard to distinguish. To help you better understand the subjective side of the scoring, I'm going to paraphrase Bill Enk, a well-respected judge for the NRHA, the National Reined Cow Horse Association (NRCHA), and the American Quarter Horse Association (AQHA). He's watched more than a few reining horses in the course of his outstanding career.

Bill explains that when you're watching a spin, if you say to yourself, "Uh-huh," with a slight nod of your head, you're probably watching a "0" performance—okay but with no significant degree of difficulty. It's correct, not really exciting, but not wrong, either. It started clean, the horse stepped around with some cadence at an average speed, and it "shut off" on the mark.

If, instead, you feel yourself smile as you nod and you say to yourself, "Yeah," you probably just saw a "+½." The horse was a bit quicker with his feet, and maintained his head and neck position while exhibiting cadence.

But if you feel actual excitement as you dip your head forward in a big nod and you say to yourself, "Now, that's what I'm talking about!" then you just saw a "+1." The horse started well and fired cleanly and quickly around, gaining speed, never losing cadence or form, and stopping precisely on the mark.

Now let's say the hair on the back of your neck prickles, your eyes get wide, and you say, "Wow!" out loud, and your eyes are *still* wide as the horse moves off into the next maneuver...chances are you've just witnessed a "+1 ½." The horse stepped smoothly right into the spin, with speed, precision, and cadence. He never waivered, but sped up til he was a blur—it seemed a horse couldn't possibly spin any faster—and then stopped perfectly on the mark. A "+1 ½" is completely flawless (and very exciting)...and quite rare to see at regular weekend shows.

Now, let's go the other way.

When you sense a slight grimace on your face, you've probably just seen a "-½." The horse stepped clumsily without precision into the spin. There was a lack of cadence and speed. The horse lost his frame or position.

### ▪ Fix It Now...and Avoid ▪ Paying the Price Later

Once you begin showing, one of your most important jobs is keeping your horse from learning to "cheat" in the show pen. (Or, if he's a seasoned horse that already knows how to cheat, you want to keep him from thinking that he can cheat with *you*.)

Horses get "show smart" amazingly quickly. If you avoid correcting them when they do something wrong during a class, they learn you're not going to get after them at a show. They become like kids in a grocery store who exhibit behavior they'd never try at home—because they know Mom isn't going to call them on it in public.

Schooling shows and "paid warm-ups" at club shows, of course, are meant for exactly this sort of schooling. But I also consider every small, inexpensive show a "potential" schooling show if it turns out my horse needs to be corrected. In other words, if he doesn't stay between the reins and remain honest, I'm going to get after him to correct it.

Most judges are well aware of the perils of showing, and if you don't abuse your horse or overdo the schooling, they'll let you continue. (And, if you stay on course, there's a chance you can still wind up the "best of the worst" that day, and place.)

So, unless there's big money at stake (not likely when you're first starting out), it's best to go ahead and school as need be during your run, especially at the beginning of your horse's show career. It will cost you some points, true, but it will also save you a lot of penalty points and frustration in the long run.

If you have an even grimmer, "Oh, no—not liver for dinner *again*!" look on your face, it's probably a "-1" performance. There was virtually no cadence, position, speed, or frame.

If you find you must force yourself to keep watching, it's probably a "-1 ½." The action bore little resemblance to a spin.

This gives you a rough idea of how scoring works, but you should also examine the rule book closely to identify potential problem areas for your horse and help you stay out of the penalty box.

## Troubleshooting Your Run

Now I'll talk about what's most likely to go wrong with your run at a show, and how to fix it at a schooling show or "paid warm-up" at a club show. (A paid warm-up is when you pay a fee to "school" in the show pen before classes begin—this is a very popular and efficient way to get show mileage on a horse while still allowing for correction in the ring.) At a regular show, our tendency is to gloss over these rough parts to maximize our score. If, however, you let him get away with too much in the show pen, he'll learn that he can "cheat" with you, and this will inevitably come back to haunt you (see sidebar).

I'm going to give you strategies for schooling your horse to correct his errors. I'll explain what your horse is most likely to do wrong, why he does it, and how to school for it to minimize his cheating in future shows.

Fidgeting in the center: By this behavior your horse is telling you he's not comfortable in the center of the pen, so you need to reassure him it's an okay place to be. If it's just that he won't stand completely still, spend a lot of time patting and reassuring him. Or, sometimes I move around a lot in the saddle, and vary the position of my rein hand to desensitize my horse. I might do this a number of times before putting any performance pressure on him. Obviously, a schooling show or a paid warm-up is the ideal place for these sorts of strategies.

If he's being really naughty—jumping up and down and pitching a little fit—put him to work right there with some suppling maneuvers. Don't make it scary or adrenaline-producing, but maybe back up around several circles with his nose and hindquarters tipped to the inside, as you learned in chapters 7 and 9 (pp. 86 and 123). Remember, backing-up is a lot of work for him, so he's not going to particularly enjoy it. Then give him the choice of standing quietly.

If, after that, he still won't stand, casually pick up the reins and back him up several circles in the other direction, then try sitting again. He'll eventually learn that when he's naughty, he has to work hard, and when he stands still in the center, he gets patted. (It usually doesn't take long for horses to figure this one out.)

When he stands quietly, go on with the pattern—but keep it relaxed and easy by avoiding speed and pressure.

Charging into the lead departure: Your horse is probably doing this because you haven't been asking correctly for your lead departure. Specifically, you haven't been picking up the reins gently, putting your horse in the correct position (with his head and hindquarters both tipped in the direction of intended movement), and making him walk that way until he's okay with it *before* loping off.

And that's also the fix in this case: if you feel your horse getting ready to jump into his lead departure, spend even more time walking quietly in "lead departure mode" before you actually move him into the lope.

Refusing to slow from the large, fast circle: Horses get carried away with themselves, and going faster is something that solves a lot of problems in the wild, so this is somewhat predictable behavior. If it happens, just pick up your reins and gradually draw your horse down to

a walk, walk a small circle or two, then lope off again. Don't make a big deal of it; remember, to the extent possible, you want slowing down to seem like a reward for your horse's hard work.

Anticipating the lead change: All horses do this! If you feel your horse starting to anticipate, set him up for the change but then just lope right through the center, without changing, and Counter-Canter around the new circle. If you do this now and then at smaller shows, your horse will be more likely to wait for your cue when it matters.

Charging through the lead change: Again, the flying lead change tends to get horses "amped" up, and sometimes their response is to pick up speed and "blow through the bridle." If you feel your horse beginning to get strong through the lead change, just pick up your reins wherever it occurs and draw him into the ground, sit for a moment, then continue on around the same circle.

Charging in the rundown: As he comes around the corner and into the rundown, your horse may start anticipating the upcoming increase in speed; if you haven't been consistent about always building your rundown speed smoothly and *gradually*, charging is almost sure to happen. Again, just shut him down as soon as you feel him taking hold of the bridle, sit for a moment, then continue.

Scotching in the rundown: He's anticipating the stop by "stutter-stopping." Chances are, you're looking down at the spot where you want to stop, which tips him off and prompts him to jump the gun. If you feel him begin to scotch, ride him all the way to the fence instead of stopping where you normally would have, then be careful to always look up, far beyond your stopping point, in the future.

Refusing to run in the rundown: This is common with lazy horses and those that have been shown a lot; it's also more common with stallions than with mares or geldings. If, when you "kiss," your horse doesn't "grab another gear," "spank" him with the rein ends and make him go all the way to the fence.

Leaning in the rundown: Your horse is refusing to stay between the reins. When this happens, change course by 30 degrees (turning him away from the direction in which he's leaning, thus overcorrecting), and continue to run straight but on your new line.

If you know your horse is going to lean toward the fence on a particular side of the arena (maybe there's a magnet there that will pull him), then go deeper into the corner and angle the rundown a bit toward the center of the arena (see fig. 11.4, p. 145).

Running crookedly in the rundown: He's "wiggling" and trying to "escape" the run because he knows the stop is next. In this case, forget the stop and "spank" him up to the fence.

Stopping crookedly: Anticipating a rollback is usually the cause. Back him up a few steps before rolling back, or even roll him the opposite way to keep him guessing the next time around.

Rolling back too soon (before a complete stop): Again, he's anticipating the rollback, probably because you haven't been consistent about letting him get all the way to the "bottom" of his stop—straight—before initiating the rollback. Let him stop all the way, back up a step or two, then roll back in the opposite direction.

Backing-up instead of rolling back: Obviously, it's easy for your horse to get confused about these two maneuvers, as your signals are so similar. If you're sure your cues and sequencing were clear (we covered this in detail in chapter 10, p. 135), then shorten up your direct rein a bit so you get more direct-rein pressure for the turn, as the neck-rein can sometimes confuse a "green-in-the-bridle" horse. (Then, at home, work on making sure your horse understands the difference between the cues for the two different maneuvers.)

Backing-up crookedly: This often happens if you don't start the backup slowly enough to be able to feel that you're straight before asking for more speed. Use your legs to straighten him out, then slowly back up a few steps (straight) before you "cluck" and ask him for more speed. (If he's never really learned how to back up straight between the reins, review the section on backing-up in chapter 8, p. 105.)

Freezing up instead of spinning: He's trying to avoid spinning or he isn't really between the reins. Move your rein hand out a bit wider, move it more slowly, shorten up the direct rein a couple of inches, and be sure your horse's nose is tipped in the direction of the spin. If that isn't enough, follow up with a tap on his shoulder from your outside foot—but *not before the nose is pointed in the right direction*, or it can become quite a mess! Also, don't let your hand get out ahead of your horse, and make him stay between the reins by using your foot to encourage his body to catch up to his face. (Then, at home, again, work on making sure he understands your cues.)

**11.5** "Hiding" from the spin
**I'm demonstrating what it looks like when a horse "hides" from the spin—that is, he turns his head away from, rather than in the direction of the spin. This can happen if he is frightened of spinning, which results from being punished at some point in a spin. This head placement can also result when you try to drag him around a spin with the reins, or if you pull your rein hand across his neck, shortening the left rein and tipping his head in the wrong direction.**

**11.6 Show goals**
Soft, relaxed, and enjoying it—that's your ultimate goal at a show. Achieve it, and everything you do, including slide stops, becomes easier and prettier. To get there, do your homework in advance, strive for a Zen-like attitude, and don't ask your horse for more than you've trained him to give.

Turning his head the wrong way in the spin: The horse is probably "hiding" from the spin out of dread of doing it (fig. 11.5). This usually happens if he's been punished in the spin (we talked about how important it is to avoid doing this, in chapter 7). He's thinking that if he doesn't put his head in the direction of the spin, he can avoid getting punished again. Use the same corrections as for freezing up, explained on p. 150.

Your horse can also turn his head the wrong way as a result of imprecise neck-reining, where your hand moves across his neck, causing the indirect rein to shorten. This pulls the horse's head to the outside. So be sure you're drawing the reins toward your turn-side belt loop, and not straight across his neck.

A "first cousin" to the above mistake is trying to speed the spin up by dragging him around with the reins. Instead, use more leg and keep your horse moving between the reins.

Spinning Too Slowly: Veteran horses are famous for spinning much more slowly in the show pen than in practice at home, probably because they know we

# AFTERWORD

I hope this book has challenged you to improve your horse and your horsemanship, whether you ride to compete or simply for enjoyment. My goal was to remove some of the "mystery" of horse training by helping you better understand these magnificent animals. If I have enabled you to establish a deeper relationship with your horse through enhanced mutual respect and two-way communication, then I'm proud to have been a part of the process.

Good luck, have fun, and keep learning!

# INDEX

Page numbers in *italic* indicate illustrations or photographs.

**Reining Essentials**